App

Disciple Building:
A Biblical Framework
with Guided Discussions

WDA®
Disciple Building

Disciple Building: A Biblical Framework with Guided Discussions
Appointing New Leaders, Phase IV-A

For copyright information:
Worldwide Discipleship Association
(Attention: Margaret Garner)
P.O. Box 142437
Fayetteville, GA 30214 USA
E-mail: mgarner@disciplebuilding.org
Web Site: www.disciplebuilding.org

In an effort to recognize that both men and women are co-heirs of God's
grace, we have chosen to use alternating gender pronouns in this document.
However, we do recognize and embrace gender-specific roles in Scripture.

Development & Writing Team:
Bob Dukes (Primary Author)
Margaret Garner
Jack Larson
Margo Theivagt

Publishing Team:
Nila Duffitt
Buddy Eades
Margaret Garner
David Parfitt

FrameworkwGD_12.02.2019
Design by Cristina van de Hoeve
Cover design by Patricia Alba-Hughes

A Welcome from WDA's President
Worldwide Discipleship Association, Inc.

Hello Friend!

Let me congratulate you on your decision to learn how to take responsibility for the spiritual well-being of others. By making this decision to continue to walk with the Lord and minister to others, you are opening yourself up to serious challenges, as well as magnificent benefits. These studies in *Disciple Building: A Biblical Framework with Guided Discussions* will help you begin to understand the phases of Christ's ministry here on earth and WDA's philosophy of ministry.

My prayer and confident belief is that "he who began a good work in you will carry it on to completion until the day of Christ Jesus" (Philippians 1:6) so that He is able "to present you before his glorious presence without fault and with great joy." (Jude 1:24)

To Him be glory and praise!

May God richly bless you as you strive to grow in Him.

Bob Dukes
President, Worldwide Discipleship Association, Inc.
Fayetteville, GA 30214

Introduction To Phase IV:
Developing New Leaders

As you begin to use the Phase IV materials, it may be useful to refer to *Maturity Matters* for a summary of this phase. The following is a synopsis.

> When a believer progresses to this phase, he is ready to take responsibility for the spiritual development and well-being of others. During this period, Jesus taught His disciples how to live in His Kingdom. In addition, He appointed The Twelve to be apostles, sending them out on their own to preach the Kingdom of God and to minister to people's needs. Mark 3:14-15 summarizes what Jesus did during this phase: "He appointed twelve [designating them apostles] that they might be with Him and that He might send them out to preach and to have authority to drive out demons."
>
> This phase actually had two parts. The first involved appointing and instructing His new leaders in Kingdom principles (Phase IV-A: Appointing New Leaders). The second involved Christ creating a series of situations that forced His leaders to reevaluate their expectations of what it meant to follow Him (Phase IV-B: Focusing On Eternal Things). Both then and now, this reevaluation crisis is pivotal. It centers on leaders choosing either the eternal benefits of following Christ or leadership roles that grant them temporal power and success. (*Maturity Matters*, pages 67-68)

For the leader who is part of the development of a young (new) leader, WDA recommends forming a discipleship group made up of people who have already completed Equipping For Ministry. (As in Jesus' ministry, this is an "invitation only" group.) These disciples would have already been able to experience and observe what it means to be "discipled" by a leader, been part of a community of Christians, and have seen and participated in ministry activities. As a result of doing ministry, these disciples will begin to identify people they wish to disciple. The discipleship leader can at this point form them into a group where they will learn and be trained while they begin to take responsibility for the spiritual development and well-being of others.

Developing a young (new) leader generally will take 6-9 months, perhaps longer depending on the time and circumstances. The first series of training will include *Living For Christ* (which includes *The Sermon On The Mount* and *Growing In Faith*), *Disciple Building: A Biblical Framework with Guided Discussions*, *A Small Groups Manual with Guided Discussions*, *Disciple Building: Life Coaching with Guided Discussion*, *Team Building* (which includes Using Spiritual Gifts), *Spiritual Warfare-II*, *How Emotional Problems Develop with Guided Discussions*, and *Kingdom Growth* which includes *Growth Of The Church* (Parables) and *Practical Outreach* (Evangelism-II). There are also Bible Readings for the disciple to use in personal devotions. WDA suggests completing the books in the order listed above. However, you may choose what works best for you in your ministry.

The second part of this training features topics related to living in the tension of the eternal versus the temporal, developing a lesson plan, teaching a topical Bible study, leading a Phase III ministry group, understanding the role of suffering, strengthening ministry principles, recognizing emotional issues, living by faith and grasping tensions within Christianity.

Disciple Building: A Biblical Framework with Guided Discussions

Table Of Contents

Leader's Instructions For Using Guided Discussions		a
Chapter 1	An Overview	1
Chapter 2	Introduction	3
Chapter 3	Five Biblical Truths	7
Chapter 4	Biblical Truth #1	9
	Because God made man in His own image, He desires that we reflect Him and bring glory to His name by growing to Christlike maturity.	
Chapter 5	Biblical Truth #2	13
	Helping Christians grow to maturity should be a top priority for the church.	
Chapter 6	Biblical Truth #3	17
	There is a process, revealed in Scripture, that produces maturity.	
Chapter 7	Biblical Truth #4	21
	Christ had a pattern/process for building disciples that can serve as the basis for a contemporary disciple building approach.	
Chapter 8	Biblical Truth #5	29
	By following Christ's pattern, we can construct a flexible framework that helps modern disciple builders develop mature disciples who can disciple others.	
Chapter 9	Balance Is Required	39
Chapter 10	Where Do We Go From Here?	47
Addendum A:	The Five Phases of Growth	49
Addendum B:	R-CAPS: Five Initiatives of a Disciple Builder	69
Addendum C:	Emotional Healing Goals of Five Phases	79
Addendum D:	Disciple Building and Classic Revivalism	91
Exhibit 1:	What Jesus Did, What We Can Do	95
Exhibit 2:	R-CAPS Grid	107
Exhibit 3:	R-CAPS Legend	111
Guided Discussions		133
Answers To The Guided Discussions		159
About WDA		169

Leader's Instructions
For Using Guided Discussions

The six Guided Discussions for *Disciple Building: A Biblical Framework with Guided Discussions* give the maturing Christian an understanding of the biblical basis of WDA's philosophy. They also give a detailed overview of Christ's ministry while He was on earth. The disciple should **read the designated pages in *Disciple Building: A Biblical Framework* <u>before</u> taking part in the Guided Discussion.**

Guided Discussions for small groups play an important role in the growth of a Christian with the **major goal being interaction around Scripture**. The goal of disciple building is not just knowledge, but Christlikeness in character and conduct. Therefore, **application is essential**. (Sections "Looking At Real Life" and "Looking at My Life" are application oriented.) At least one-third of the small group discussion time should be spent discussing application of the truth. It is often tempting to get caught up in the content part of the study, but you, as the leader, are responsible to move the group along to application.

If you have used WDA materials before, you may remember that we often have Pocket Principles® for you to read before the group discussion. In this study the "Pocket Principle™" is a book, specifically *Disciple Building: A Biblical Framework*, written by Bob Dukes, President of WDA, and published by WDA. You will be given sections of this book to read before the Group Discussion. Because our Pocket Principle™ is a book, there are no Teaching Outlines.

Unlike WDA materials in Phases I, II, and III, these materials have only <u>one</u> (1) version, not separate leader and student versions. You will find the notes to the leader and the answers to the Guided Discussion questions in the back of the book. Leaders need to read these notes and the answers before the meeting where the specific lesson will be discussed. There they will find suggestions, cautions, and additional helpful information.

Much of the preparation has been done for you as a leader: topics and Scriptures have been chosen, and questions written. However, it is important that you become comfortable with the material so that you will be able to be flexible and focus on the needs of your group. In *A Small Groups Manual* (WDA), you will find information about the practical aspects of group leadership. Please refer to the section titled "Practical Dynamics of Small Group Leadership." This is available from the WDA store at www.disciplebuilding.org/store/leadership-manuals/a-small-groups-manual-paperback.

Chapter 1
An Overview

This book provides a biblical strategy for helping Christians grow to maturity. Maturity is defined as becoming increasingly conformed to the likeness of Jesus Christ. Maturity is a process, and it is progressive. As people obey the truths of Scripture, they increase their understanding of God and His Kingdom. As this occurs, God gradually changes the Christians' conduct, belief systems, worldview, and ultimately, their character. Maturity also produces an increased capacity for deepening our relationship with God and others, with agape (sacrificial) love as the ultimate outcome.

The process of disciple building (teaching Christians to obey all that Christ commanded) is central to His commission to the church and, therefore, should be a priority for Christian leaders. For a number of reasons, the modern church has not developed and implemented effective disciple building approaches. Fortunately, we can remedy this situation. But the solution, though simple, is not simplistic. We must understand, balance, and apply all the dynamics that affect progressive growth. This will be challenging, but rewarding. Major themes include:

- We face a worldwide crisis of maturity.

- People need to grow.

- We need a new perspective regarding disciple building.

- Building disciples requires wisdom and balance.

There are Five Biblical Truths that support biblical disciple building:

Biblical Truth #1: Because God made man in His own image, He desires that we reflect Him and bring glory to His name by growing to Christlike maturity.

Biblical Truth #2: Helping Christians grow to maturity should be a top priority for the church.

Biblical Truth #3: There is a process, revealed in Scripture, that produces maturity.

Biblical Truth #4: Christ had a pattern/process for building disciples that can serve as the basis for a contemporary disciple building approach.

Biblical Truth #5: By following Christ's pattern, we can construct a flexible framework that helps modern disciple builders develop mature disciples who can disciple others.

Chapter 2
Introduction

WE FACE A WORLDWIDE CRISIS OF CHARACTER AND MATURITY

In 970 BC, King Solomon of Israel was the most powerful and wealthy ruler in the entire world. He was the heir of beloved King David, who wholeheartedly loved God, the creator of heaven and earth. The royal city of Jerusalem became the desired destination of envoys from around the world as rulers sought an audience with the "wisest man on earth."

But as his power and wealth increased, Solomon's heart toward God was compromised. After his death, his dynasty gradually declined and degenerated. Though retaining an outward allegiance to God, future rulers and the people who followed them were inwardly filled with greed, corruption, and rebellion.

God repeatedly offered grace and forgiveness, urging them to turn their hearts back to Him. Instead, they abandoned worship of the one true God and served foreign gods. Ultimately, they grew weary of hearing God's Word altogether, and murdered His spokesmen, the prophets of The Old Testament.

In response, God allowed cruel foreigners to conquer them, ransack their capital, tear down the city wall, and destroy the Temple built by Solomon centuries earlier. In fulfillment of prophecy, King Nebuchadnezzar invaded, plundered their land, and exiled the people of God into captivity in Babylon. When national character declines, nations topple. For 70 years Palestine languished, and Jerusalem, the wall, her people, and the Temple lay in ruins.

In the course of time, the Babylonian Empire was conquered by Persia, and Nehemiah, a Jewish exile, was appointed an official in the court of Artaxerxes. This cupbearer to the king, a man of great character, was anointed by God to lead one of the greatest restoration projects in history! Recognizing that the days of the Jewish exile were completed but that Jerusalem was still in ruins, Nehemiah, exercising great courage, rallied a remnant of God's people to return to Israel to rebuild the city and its walls.

Armed with a deep conviction that fueled fervent prayer, Nehemiah led a historic rebuilding campaign that fostered restoration and recovery and spawned a national revival. In a mere 52 days, amid great hardship, danger, and sacrifice, the city was fortified, allowing commerce and government to flourish once again. Another golden age of Jewish history ensued as godly character and wisdom replaced compromise, and hope displaced despair.

Currently Christianity, once a fortress of spiritual strength, faces a growing crisis as we witness the breakdown of the structures that have historically fostered morality and character. Our families have fragmented amid selfish individualism fueled by consumer-oriented societies. Our schools have exchanged biblical values for secular humanistic philosophies and mysticism. Governments seem confused, wondering if there is a foundation of absolutes upon which to establish law and policy, or if shifting public opinion should shape public life. And if that isn't enough, the media seems bent on pulling down what remains of a biblical worldview. Are we living, as Dickens observed in *A Tale of Two Cities*, in the "worst of times"? The nightly news seems to be evidence enough.

Underlying this crisis in society is a crisis of character.

Though it may seem that these problems emerged overnight, this character crisis has actually been developing for some time and can be linked to a blind spot in Christianity. For many years, the church has failed to produce men and women of character in significant numbers. Without leaders of character, societies ultimately decline, and eventually fail. Many of our churches have abandoned a biblical worldview altogether, and others have neglected spiritual nurture for programs in which success is determined primarily by numbers, effectively sacrificing maturity for members.

Ironically, we live in a culture that is filled with spiritual needs but is growing increasingly hostile toward evangelical Christianity. Christianity is progressively ceasing to be "salt and light" to the world, and is in danger of being "trampled underfoot by men." But there is good news!

God is not unaware or indifferent. He is sovereign over the nations (Psalm 2) and Lord of His church, and He will defend the honor of His name and renew His people. Throughout history, when it seemed as if the people of God were surely defeated, the troubles they faced often became the catalyst for renewal and victory. Sometimes it requires hardship and defeat to refocus our perspective. Romans 8:28-29 affirms that, "God causes all things to work together for good to those who love God, to those who are called according to His purpose. For those whom He foreknew, He also predestined to become conformed to the image of His Son." (NASB)

Helping people become Christlike is not easy. There are obstacles. The way is difficult, at times hard-to-understand, and it requires humility and faith. But the outcome is worth it, both for now and for eternity. We must be honest. Current approaches for helping Christians grow to maturity are not working adequately.

We need a new approach, a new perspective. Any new perspective requires a new way of thinking. This in itself is challenging for some. And it will require biblical balance. The growth process involves both mystery and method. God is in charge, but He expects us to do our part. He is building a people for His own pleasure who are able to rise above the world, take on the characteristics of God Himself, and live significant lives that impact all eternity. Like the courageous leader Nehemiah, we need a proper perspective of His plans and strategies to fully appreciate the process He has designed to accomplish His objectives.

A PROPER PERSPECTIVE PROVIDES HOPE

Three men digging a ditch on a scorching summer afternoon were approached by a friend who asked, "What are you guys doing?" The first, already weary from exertion, responded impatiently, "What does it look like? We're digging a hole!" The second, sensing that the question was not meant to be rhetorical, added, "We're laying a foundation pad. It's going to be filled with concrete."

The third man, who had been whistling happily while he labored, laid his shovel aside, wiped his forehead, and began to describe in great detail how this particular hole was strategic for the placement of one of the massive flying buttresses that would support an entire wall of stained glass windows for a new cathedral. After describing in great detail the plans and procedures for completion of the structure, which was sure to take several years, he added, "If things go according to plan, on Christmas Eve five years from now my family and I will worship together at the altar where that rubbish pile is now located."

All three men were working hard at the same task. But their attitudes varied markedly depending on their perspective. The man who maintained the most comprehensive perspective had the best attitude and the most energy. Having a proper perspective enables us to survey a situation and see not just what is happening, but the significance behind what is happening, and the capacity to develop strategies for what needs to happen next.

The root causes behind our current crisis are complex, but as Christians we must shoulder some of the responsibility. Though individual Christians and some communities have found ways to grow and develop, on a large scale the church has lost some of the capacity to be salt and light in the world. We have not, as the Scriptures command, made growth toward spiritual maturity a primary goal. Disciple building has broken down. When disciple building breaks down, cultures soon follow.

We are again at a pivot-point in history. Will we complacently live amid the rubble of our crumbling societies or, like Nehemiah, rise and rebuild the walls? It will depend upon our perspective of God and His Kingdom. Without such a vision, it might be easy to lose hope and become weary in this difficult hour. Are we merely "digging ditches" or are we building something wonderful "to the glory of God"?

Chapter 3
Five Biblical Truths

What difference do you think it would make if more of the Christians in your community began behaving more like Christ? If, instead of squabbling over minor issues of doctrine or breaking fellowship over matters of style, they exhibited charity as they deferred to one another? What if more Christians trusted God to clarify matters as they patiently waited in prayer, even if this meant that they had to lose an argument or assume a less prominent role? What if honesty and integrity were the hallmark of every business transaction among Christians? What if evangelism included more "doing of good works for the public good," extensions of a good God who "sends rain on the righteous and the unrighteous"? (Matthew 5:45)

Such changes of conduct and character would be significant, to say the least. Now multiply that impact for all the places Christians are located around the world, and you begin to understand God's agenda! Maturity does make a difference! Jesus said, "but everyone, after he has been fully trained, will be like his teacher." (Luke 6:40) He then instructed His disciples to teach His new followers "to obey everything" (Matthew 28:20) He commanded. For this to occur, a plan is needed: a plan for teaching everything (a curriculum) and a plan for encouraging obedience to truth (an application process).

WDA has developed such a process. In fact, it's the same approach Jesus used. He taught truth relationally, gradually and progressively as He exhorted His followers to obey. He also challenged them to assume appropriate ministry responsibilities, and prayed that their faith would grow and their relationship with God and each other would deepen. Ultimately, the quality of bold (agape) love is the final outcome and evidence of a relationship with Him (John 13:33-34).

One goal of this book is to communicate an approach that helps disciple builders devise growth strategies for people they want to encourage toward maturity in Christ. This process is not easy. It involves more than just understanding concepts. It requires sacrifice and devotion derived from a strongly held conviction that the task is important, even imperative. A careful study of Scripture, condensed into five biblical truths, helps provide this conviction.

Chapter 4
Biblical Truth #1

Because God made man in His own image, He desires that we
reflect Him and bring glory to His name by growing to
Christlike maturity.

Many items on our public agenda reflect the confusion that exists
regarding our understanding of who we are. This is not just a
contemporary dilemma. The psalmist framed the same question:
"What is man, that Thou art mindful of him?" (Psalm 8:4, KJV)
And modern man still wonders: "Are humans just 'tissue' that has
evolved by chance and natural selection, or are we something more
noble?" Scripture affirms that we are reflections of our Creator,
beings with a purpose. Christians hold to the conviction that we
were created in the image of God to reflect His glory (Genesis 1:26-
27). Other principles related to a Biblical view of man include:

- **God's image in man is marred because of sin and the
  Fall.** This is more than a biblical observation. Countless wars,
  injustices, and inhumanities are evidence that something is
  wrong with the human race (Genesis 3:1-7).

- **Man is both dignified and depraved.** Though corrupted by
  sin, we still retain remnants of the divine image. In spite of our
  bent toward destroying the planet and everything on it, we are
  still capable of producing great works of art, tremendous feats
  of engineering, and demonstrating kindness and compassion
  (James 3:9.)

- **Christ is the Second Adam.** He came to seek and save that
  which was lost, and He has secured redemption and ultimate
  restoration for His followers (Romans 8:29-30; I Corinthians
  15:45-49).

- **Christlikeness, or maturity, is God's goal for His people.**
  Irenaus, one of the early church fathers, summed up God's
  intent by declaring: "The glory of God, is man fully alive."
  Jesus said He came to give life "to the full!" (John 10:10 cf.
  Romans 8:29-30)

Being made fully alive in Christ, set apart and gradually changed
for God's purposes and glory, is referred to by theologians as
sanctification. The process of our sanctification includes, among other
things, the mandate given to the church to teach disciples to observe
all that Christ commanded (Matthew 28:19-20). Disciple building,
central to the process of conforming us to the likeness of Christ, is
therefore, at the heart of God's purpose for mankind.

PEOPLE NEED AND WANT TO GROW

God wants His people to progress to maturity, and Christians
want to grow up. What is most needed is a better understanding
and application of the growth process. The church today needs to
find a more effective way to develop mature lay leadership that is
able to work alongside the vocational church staff to equip others
in the congregation. Paul refers to this process in his ministry and
instruction to Timothy:

*And the things you have heard me say in the presence of many witnesses,
entrust to reliable men who will also be qualified to teach others.*
(II Timothy 2:2)

Paul had been discipling Timothy, and now he wanted Timothy to
have a similar ministry with "reliable" men who would be able to
disciple others. It was Paul's clear goal to multiply himself and his
ministry through Timothy. Moreover, Paul instructs the churches to
have this same kind of ministry in the church as a whole.

*It was He (Jesus) who gave some to be apostles, some to be prophets, some to
be evangelists, and some to be pastors and teachers, to prepare God's people for
works of service, so that the body of Christ may be built up until we all reach
unity in the faith and in the knowledge of the Son of God and become mature,
attaining to the whole measure of the fullness of Christ.* (Ephesians 4:11-13)

Paul's message is clear: church leaders, using their gifts, must assume responsibility to disciple people in the congregation so that they are able to minister to others. Then as the congregation develops, the whole church becomes involved in building itself up. This is necessary for the whole church to reach unity and maturity and impact the world.

WE NEED A NEW PERSPECTIVE REGARDING DISCIPLE BUILDING

The plan is not complicated, but there is an important unanswered question. "What is the pattern or process by which the church leadership is to train and instruct others in the congregation?" Paul refers to a "pattern of sound teaching" in his instructions to Timothy (II Timothy 1:13). Where can we find this pattern that enables church leaders to develop character and produce maturity? Must the modern church use "trial and error" to figure it out? Will the Spirit of God lead us? Are we to simply teach the Scriptures and trust that character will develop? God will certainly use many means to equip us, but what if there is a more strategic method? As we will see, Jesus Himself provided such a disciple building approach.

Chapter 5
Biblical Truth #2

Helping Christians grow to maturity should be a top priority
for the church.

A friend jokingly tells the story of two grounds keepers. After one dug
a hole, the other filled it up. A puzzled bystander approached them
for an explanation for this seemingly bizarre behavior. "It's simple,"
one replied. "The guy who *plants* the trees is sick today!" Though
admittedly a bit corny, this story illustrates the state of affairs in much
of Christian ministry in this century. Hard work and organization
aren't enough if we leave out an important component of our mission.

WE MUST COMPLETELY FULFILL THE GREAT COMMISSION

Jesus said, "Go therefore and make disciples of all nations, baptizing
them in the name of the Father and the Son and the Holy Spirit,
teaching them to observe all that I commanded you; and lo, I am with
you always, even to the end of the age." (Matthew 28:19-20, NASB,
emphasis added)

Many in the modern church seem to have forgotten, or neglected,
this component of the Commission given by Christ. This Commission
to extend the Kingdom rule of Christ throughout the earth is more
than an evangelistic mandate. It also includes the training (discipling,
equipping, nurturing) of Christians to apply all the teachings of
Christ. We need a balanced view of the Kingdom to appreciate what
Christ is commanding us to do in His name. Our Lord's Commission
to make disciples (mature followers) extends to today's church leaders
and includes two key principles governing this process:

- A mandate to teach a complete, **definitive body of truth** to all
  Christians.

- A mandate to teach the **application of truth** (versus the
  retention of truth only).

The Scriptures present the saving mission of Christ (His Kingdom) in three components:

1. He came to justify us by His substitutionary death and give us forgiveness of sin so that we might be accepted as children of God (Justification).

2. He came to be the Lord of our lives and (through the power of the Holy Spirit) deliver us from Satan's grasp, remake us morally into His image, and enable us to love one another. His reign is extended into our hearts, where He is gradually changing our character and conduct into His likeness (Sanctification).

3. Ultimately He will return in power and glory, totally deliver us from all evil and transform our fallen world into a new world where righteousness dwells (Glorification).

During the Reformation, Protestant Christianity recovered the doctrines of grace related to our justification. Spreading the good news of forgiveness and acceptance through faith in Christ's death and resurrection became paramount. The doctrine of works (good deeds) as the basis for our justification was rightly rejected. But the Protestant churches never fully developed a strategy that integrated works (part of sanctification) into the Protestant framework of the Christian life.

The emphasis on the first component of the Kingdom increased among those who would later become known as the evangelicals/ fundamentalists (i.e. those who held to divine inspiration of Scriptures, the deity of Christ and His future reign, and stressed the evangel/good news of Christ's sacrifice for sins and the fundamentals of the faith). During the 19th century, these conservatives moved away from issues championed by the rising liberal movement within the church. But the liberal agenda included many issues related to disciple building (e.g. social development, good works, personal growth).

Consequently, some conservative Christians tend to place less emphasis on these issues, choosing instead to focus on the message of justification and the coming reign of Christ. Sadly, the disciple building issues have never fully re-emerged as priorities for many in the evangelical community. This has led to a situation where many who profess Christ still live defeated lives. Rather than growing to maturity, they are still ensnared by old habits and patterns of sin. We must return to a balanced emphasis. We must recapture biblical disciple building and press on to maturity.

The Nottingham Statement, drafted by the Second Evangelical Anglican Congress in 1977, sums up the meaning of maturity:

Becoming mature in Christ involves both the deepening of our relationship with Him in repentance, faith and obedience, and the transforming into His likeness, which includes our thinking, behavior, attitudes, habits, and character. Together with growth in the knowledge of God and His truth, there should be a development in the capacity to distinguish between good and evil. The supreme glory of this maturing is the increasing ability to love and be loved in our relationship with God, the Church and the world. This transformation is accomplished by the action of the Holy Spirit, using the means of grace.

DISCIPLE BUILDING SHOULD BE A PRIORITY BECAUSE GOD COMMANDS IT.

Developing a process for growth that produces maturity is a big order. But since God commands it we can expect that He will provide the wisdom to accomplish the task. In fact, the discovery process itself serves to develop our character and leads to more significant leadership responsibility. Scripture hints at this dynamic in the Book of Proverbs where it asserts: "It is the glory of God to conceal a matter, but the glory of kings is to search out a matter." (Proverbs 25:2, NASB) WDA has been studying the disciple building process for many years, seeking to discover a biblical pattern that produces maturity. We are confident that such a process exists. And as we will see, Jesus provided just such a process!

DISCIPLE BUILDING SHOULD BE A PRIORITY BECAUSE OF THE BLESSINGS THAT ACCOMPANY IT.

It is helpful to be reminded that godliness (the outcome of disciple building) actually produces incredible blessings, both in this age and in the age that is coming (I Timothy 4:8; I Timothy 6:6). Jesus repeatedly urged His disciples to "not work for food that spoils, but for food that endures to eternal life." (John 6:27) Scripture is filled with such admonitions offered to encourage us to persevere (cf. Hebrews 5:14; II Peter 1:10; I Corinthians 3:10-15).

While it is true that even the most basic act of faith opens the gates of heaven and ushers Christians into Paradise, Scripture also affirms the rewards of faithfulness and obedience that enhance our citizenship in Heaven. Unfortunately, many Evangelicals are taught to focus on heaven as the blessing of salvation, but are not instructed thoroughly regarding the conditions that produce many of the blessings of heaven. Most of these conditional blessings are directly linked to mature obedience, outcomes of disciple building (Romans 2:6-10; II Peter 1:10-11; Matthew 25: 21; II Timothy 4:7-8).

Chapter 6
Biblical Truth #3

There is a process, revealed in Scripture, that produces maturity.

Actually, growth to maturity occurs throughout life. It starts when we are born and begins to develop in our family of origin, and ends when we die and/or see Christ face-to-face. Some believe this panoramic perspective of the maturing process was what John the Apostle was referring to in I John 2:12-14 when he mentioned "little children, young men, and fathers." This would make sense. There seem to be three broad developmental periods of life that contribute to our becoming mature. In summary:

1. **The Formative Years in the Home**: This is the period that takes place in our family of origin from the time we are born until we depart from home and the family that raised us. (As we will see later, what happens to us in childhood has a profound effect on later growth.) This is the stage when our character is initially formed. Christians are not the only ones who develop godly character in children. Because man is made in God's image, even non-Christians can instill honesty, integrity, industry, discipline, etc. And some Christian homes may teach biblical truth, but still fail to provide a healthy environment for building relationships or fostering secure emotional foundations. This is ironic, but true nonetheless.

2. **Young Adulthood**: This is the period from late childhood "until Christ is formed" in us (Galatians 4:19) and we become "mature and complete, not lacking anything." (James 1:4) Certainly this doesn't mean we have stopped growing, but that we have reached adulthood and have been equipped with all the tools and experiences needed to function as mature adults. I am convinced this is the period where we must complete the training begun in the home and teach Christians to obey all that Christ commanded. For those who progress normally, this

occurs from late adolescence (age 14-24) until early adulthood (age 24-34). For those who have experienced developmental problems, or who have not been adequately equipped in childhood, this stage can remain unfinished well into adult life, perhaps never being completed.

3. **Mature Adulthood**: This is the period that starts after we have been equipped as mature disciples and lasts until we die, or meet Christ. It occurs after we have been trained to put all His commands into practice. In other words, this stage of development builds on the previous stage. It doesn't mean that we have "fully arrived," or that we don't need further growth and the application of truth. It does mean that we have the capacity to age gracefully and maturely because we have been trained to discern good from evil and taught to live well in a fallen world.

The goal of developing mature, godly character is complex and difficult to achieve, due in part to the fact that we are complex beings made in God's image, and in part to the fact that there are enemies that hinder the process. Another reason for the difficulty stems from the fact that Christians do not always agree on how growth occurs, what is required to produce this growth, or what role church leaders should assume in facilitating growth. While most evangelicals are committed to disciple building, not everyone defines the process in the same way.

NEEDED: A CLARIFICATION AND DEFINITION OF TERMS

Sometimes when discipleship is mentioned, people think of inflexible study programs or rigorous accountability. Others insist there is no definitive process of spiritual development, because everybody is unique. For these, discipleship involves unpredictability. Others think of discipleship as the "follow-up" (assimilation and teaching) that needs to occur just after conversion. Someone else might define discipleship as "spiritual formation" and mean anything from discovering spiritual gifts, mastering spiritual disciplines, or embracing a mystical experience. Unfortunately, other definitions come to mind for some, those whose experience involved more manipulation than equipping.

Because of the confusion regarding the term "discipleship," we prefer to use the term "disciple building" to refer to: "That intentional process, entrusted to the church as part of Christ's Commission, and set forth as a priority in Scripture, where more mature leaders come alongside less mature Christians and help them grow to Christlike maturity. This process includes teaching them to obey all that Christ commanded, and equipping them to train others also."

FIVE CHARACTERISTICS OF A BIBLICAL DISCIPLE BUILDING APPROACH

Disciple building involves human programs, but it must allow room for God to remain in control, and it must recognize all of the complexities and dynamics involved in spiritual growth. This balance is difficult to achieve, requiring wisdom and a biblical understanding of sanctification. For this reason, we must not settle for an approach that fails to recognize and embrace all of the following characteristics:

1. **Disciple building must be flexible.**

   One size does NOT fit all. People are complex, created in His image. We have different needs, learning styles, and personalities. There are other variables that also affect growth (environment, culture, the impact of abuse, biblical literacy, etc.). Maintaining flexibility requires wisdom (Colossians 1:28-29). There is also an interplay of different growth agents. God is involved; the church has a role; and every individual Christian should assume responsibility for his own growth.

2. **Disciple building must be progressive.**

   Maturity takes place over time, not overnight. We grow from less mature to more mature. People need to understand simpler truths in order to comprehend more complex truths. Truth must be experienced (put into practice) to be fully understood.

3. **Disciple building must integrate the equipping of leaders with helping everyone achieve emotional and relational health.**

   All Christians need to grow as leaders (in some capacity). All Christians have been damaged by sin (some more than others) and need healing and restoration.

4. **Disciple building must be purposeful: producing Christlike maturity.**

   It must help us become holy, because God is holy, impacting our walk of faith and dependency on God, affecting our worldview and values. It must influence and change our conduct and character. It must help us realize our true identity. It must impact our relationships, ultimately producing the quality of bold, sacrificial love for God and others.

5. **Disciple building must be transferable.**

   It must be transferable to others who can also pass it on. It must be able to adapt itself to various settings, cultures, and contexts. It must simplify a complex process without robbing the process of its complexity. It must be rendered visually because people need to be able to see something to build it. Whenever practical, it must utilize existing resources and structures within the established community of faith. It must integrate all biblical expressions of ministry. It must WORK, practically, for busy people.

Chapter 7
Biblical Truth #4

Christ had a pattern/process for building disciples that can serve as the basis for a contemporary disciple building approach.

Jesus had a plan for accomplishing His disciple building training, and that plan was transferred to His apostles. Christ's disciple building included more than evangelistic reproduction; it involved the development of character and followed a pattern that produced gradual growth and maturation.

Peter echoed Christ's teaching, urging progressively building faith, until the ultimate goal of agape (Christlike) love is attained (II Peter 1:5-9). Paul urged Timothy to reproduce the "pattern of sound teaching" in others and reminded him that the goal of this instruction was agape love (II Timothy 1:5,13-14, 2:2). John addressed three distinct groups as children, young men, and fathers (illustrating stages of spiritual growth) and taught that professions of faith without obedience and love are hypocritical (I John 2:12-14, 2:3-6).

THE GOSPELS AS A GUIDE

The only place in Scripture where a progressive ministry model is fully developed is in the description of the ministry of Jesus Christ given in the Gospels. When we look at the Epistles we only get a snapshot of what is happening in a particular situation at a particular point in time. There is no progression in the Epistles. The book of Acts shows progression in the spread of the gospel, but there is not enough detail regarding what was done at any one location to give us a specific pattern to observe and follow. But in the Gospels we see Christ equipping His followers (in particular The Twelve) from their initial belief in Him to a point of maturity where He was able to leave a fledgling church in their hands.

Jesus prepared His disciples to have a ministry of their own under the power and guidance of the Holy Spirit. The Gospels show what

He taught and the order in which He presented it. Luke 10 and the following chapters preserve what Jesus taught The Seventy: material nearly identical to what He taught The Twelve. We see that Jesus taught truths in a certain order for the progressive growth of each follower from his first call until He left them. This pattern brought Jesus' disciples to a greater commitment and trust in Him and a readiness for ministry.

The Scriptures contain four Gospels, four different perspectives of our Lord's life and ministry, underscoring the importance of a comprehensive view. By integrating the four Gospels into one document organized chronologically, Biblical scholars provided a helpful tool for studying the life and ministry of Christ. This *Harmony of the Gospels* affords a progressive look at how Jesus conducted His ministry and trained His disciples.

At the conclusion of His ministry on earth, Jesus tells His disciples to repeat what He did. This would have been natural because we all tend to train others by relying on our own experience. But Jesus' final Commission was for our benefit too, reminding us to look to the Gospels as a pattern for training. There are other solid reasons for studying the Gospels as the basis for a modern pattern of building disciples. Whether we look to the Gospels for our disciple building pattern or not, the church is still under obligation from the Great Commission to figure out what Jesus did and repeat it.

After forty years of study and application of this process, WDA has concluded that there is a repeatable process revealed in Scripture that produces maturity. Our goal here is not to be exhaustive, but to show some of the main goals and methods of Jesus that can be utilized today. Rather than unpack the day-to-day activities of Jesus, we are looking for trends and pivot-points. We ask strategic questions regarding what Jesus did to equip His disciples.

People can fail to see the themes of disciple building in the Gospels because they don't look at them with the equipping of the original disciples in mind. Dr. Robert Coleman was one of the pioneers of the modern disciple building movement. In his book *The Master Plan of Evangelism*, Coleman makes the observation that everything Jesus did was done with The Twelve in mind. In one sense, the worldwide extension of Christ's Kingdom rule depended upon the equipping of The Twelve. They were in the background of nearly everything Jesus said and did. WDA's Founder, Carl Wilson, expands this theme in *With Christ in the School of Disciple Building*.

Once you realize the priority of equipping The Twelve, the entire account of Jesus' life takes on a new perspective. If we begin with the assumption that much of what Jesus did was primarily for the benefit of The Twelve, it changes how we view His ministry. In every situation we should ask, "How does this affect The Twelve?" Certainly, what Jesus did had a broader impact, but what He did with The Twelve most certainly changed them and prepared them for leading the church.

A careful study of the ministry of our Lord, using a *Harmony of the Gospels* as a guide, reveals five distinct phases of His disciple building ministry. Each phase marks a major shift in the emphasis of His training ministry. In order to better understand the process of helping others grow, in each of these phases we seek to answer several questions:

- What was His focus in teaching His disciples?

- How did His relationship with the disciples develop and change?

- What did He pray for His followers?

- How did He train them for ministry?

- What activities or situations did He construct to stretch their faith?

- How did He meet their emotional and relational needs?

THE FIVE PHASES OF DISCIPLE BUILDING

Growth does not occur overnight. Just as a newborn baby develops gradually and only after much nourishment and the proper care, so it is with the "babe" in Christ—the new Christian. We should expect to drink milk before we can eat meat, and to crawl before we can walk. God understands this better than we do, and He patiently works with us as He conforms us to the image of His Son. Again, we see this principle illustrated in the approach Christ took with His disciples.

Christ was deliberate in the way that He related to and worked with His disciples. Because each of the Gospel writers recorded the life of Christ from his own perspective, it can be difficult to see a pattern simply by reading through the New Testament. But a *Harmony of the Gospels* reveals that Jesus taught His disciples things that were appropriate for each phase of growth, and that He moved them through successive phases. It is also clear that Jesus intended this pattern to be repeated. Before His return to heaven, He commanded His followers to make disciples in all nations, teaching the same things He had taught. A brief overview of the Five Phases of Christ's disciple building ministry is listed below. (For a more complete analysis, including flow and progression and an expanded description of the patterns and themes: see Addendum A and Exhibits 1, 2 and 3.)

PHASE I: ESTABLISHING FAITH

John the Baptist and Jesus called people to change their minds about their life of sin and begin a new life through faith in God. They warned of the coming judgment and talked about the meaning of sin. They taught about God's love and His forgiveness of the sinner. Jesus was revealed as the Lamb of God who takes away the sins of the world. Many were converted and turned from their selfish, sinful lives to trust God and the promised Messiah.

PHASE II: LAYING FOUNDATIONS

Jesus called a group of disciples to be with Him and helped them understand His super-natural and heavenly origin evidenced by His miracles. He taught them that He was the Messiah and showed them His deity and power— that of the glorious Son of God. As they developed a personal relationship with Him, they learned that there was continued acceptance and forgiveness through Him. They shared their new faith with others and learned to follow Him obediently. They began to relate to each other as fellow Christians.

PHASE III: EQUIPPING FOR MINISTRY

Jesus called some of His disciples to be "fishers-of-men." They committed themselves to minister with Him publicly, and He took them with Him in His evangelism campaigns. He taught them the principles of evangelism, showed them His love for the sinner and demonstrated His power to forgive sin and give new life. He established His power over evil and His authority to judge all men and to justify the Christian at the resurrection. He taught them about some of the differences between the two spiritual kingdoms, preparing them for the realities of spiritual warfare. He reinforced the importance of grace as the foundation of a relationship with God.

PHASE IV: DEVELOPING NEW LEADERS

After spending the entire night in prayer, Jesus chose The Twelve as leaders. He organized His Kingdom around this new group, instructing them and giving them authority. His teaching focused on His new Kingdom: its blessings and the new law of inner righteousness. He contrasted the Kingdom of heaven with Satan's and used parables to teach The Twelve how God's Kingdom would grow. Jesus showed His disciples that He was not offering merely a better life in this world, but eternal life—everlasting life of the highest quality. He precipitated a faith-crisis, causing them to reevaluate their expectations and trust God for the eternal things of life above the temporal. Jesus challenged the status quo, revealing Himself again as the Lord from heaven. He taught divine authority over human authority and proclaimed assurance of eternal life and future glory.

PHASE V: DEVELOPING MATURE LEADERS

As His fame and ministry grew, Jesus appointed seventy other leaders to assist Him. The original Twelve assumed increased responsibility and ownership of the mission. They learned to trust Him to work in other members of the body and to cope with outside opposition. He taught them about evils that would harm the Christian life. As The Twelve assumed new responsibilities, they became self-reliant. They discovered through the crucifixion and the resurrection that human flesh was inadequate for the Christian life. They learned of God's sovereignty and the all-sufficiency of Christ in and through His Holy Spirit. They learned that His Kingdom was not confined to Israel, but extended worldwide. He commissioned them to make disciples of all nations. They were to transfer the same training they had received to others, urging these new disciples to obediently follow Him.

THE FIVE INITIATIVES OF A DISCIPLE BUILDER: R-CAPS

After Christ left earth, He sent the Spirit to gradually make His followers more like Christ. This process occurs through disciple building and is made effective in the lives of Christians by the gracious initiatives of a God who is sovereign over the entire process. Paul refers to this balance of human initiative and God-orchestrated results when he reminded the Corinthians that he and Apollos planted and watered but that it was God who was causing the growth. Apart from the grace of God, no spiritual life is possible: "For it is by grace you have been saved, through faith—and this not from yourselves, it is the gift of God—not by works, so that no one can boast." (Ephesians 2:8-9) God is the One who causes growth, but He entrusts to people the task of disciple building as a critical part of the spiritual growth process.

People who want to help others grow need to understand both the progression of spiritual maturation and the means-of-grace (See *Nottingham Statement*, Chapter 5), or growth initiatives, available to a disciple builder. It is important to know where a disciple is along a progressive growth continuum and be able to employ five growth initiatives to facilitate effective growth and development.

We already have seen that Christ trained His disciples according to a specific pattern of spiritual development. Jesus, under the power and guidance of the Spirit, repeatedly engaged in five activities to help His disciples grow:

1. He built **relationships** with them, connecting appropriately and strategically.

2. He taught them **content** (truth about God and His Kingdom) and trained them in skills.

3. He provided **accountability**, encouraging them to put truth into practice.

4. He spent time in **prayer** for them, often fighting spiritual battles.

5. He placed them in **situations** that challenged them to greater commitment and faith.

   (For more on the Five Initiatives: see Addendum B and Exhibits 1, 2 and 3)

Chapter 8
Biblical Truth #5

By following Christ's pattern, we can construct a flexible framework that helps modern disciple builders develop mature disciples who can disciple others.

People who want to help others grow know they must depend on God to help; but they also sense that He expects them to assume responsibility and take the initiative. Whether a college student in a campus ministry, a Sunday School teacher, a pastor, or a parent, when it comes to getting started, questions arise for disciple builders:

- Where do I begin?

- How do I know what someone really needs?

- Is there a way of tracking spiritual maturity?

- Is there a growth process?

- What causes growth to occur?

- How do I help someone take the next step?

- What if I run into problems?

- What materials should I use, and where can I find them?

- Are they appropriate for this person?

- Are they practical?

- Are they affordable?

- Is there a way to provide structure without a rigid program?

There is a process of growth to maturity in Christ, revealed in Scripture. Though mysterious in some ways, it's also practical and manageable for those who want to help others grow, or grow themselves. We are all unique, but we all grow. Though every child is different, all children develop similarly, growing in stages and needing nourishment and care. In the same way, spiritual children are unique, but they too grow up gradually, progressing according to God's prescribed stages of development (Hebrews 5:12-14; I John 2:12-14). (Unfortunately, like natural development, spiritual growth can be stunted or delayed unless proper care is provided. More about this later.)

As we have seen, Jesus had a plan for building mature leaders for the church and equipping them to train others to put His commands into practice. Employing five initiatives and following a progressive pattern, He laid the foundation for intentional disciple building that would change the world. By studying His ministry approach, we can help modern Christians grow to maturity, becoming salt and light in a dark world.

Once we understand the specific initiatives (means-of-grace) that Jesus used to stimulate growth and the progressive pattern of spiritual development, we can construct a growth framework or grid that helps us understand how to help someone else grow. By using this framework, we are able to prayerfully design projects that, under the power of the Spirit, will help our disciples grow to maturity. This framework of spiritual development, the R-CAPS Grid (derived from an acronym of the five initiatives), can be used as a practical tool for disciple building.

Understanding how spiritual growth occurs enables leaders to stay in step with the Spirit by anticipating the normal process of development that He has created. There is room for our wise planning alongside His sovereign initiation and control. By focusing on what to teach, how to relate and how to pray for the disciples (etc.), according to their level of maturity, we don't over or under-challenge them, but meet them where they are. Programs are involved, but they are programs strategically designed to help people grow to Christlike maturity.

Rather than being rigid, this approach allows us to change what we do to help a disciple grow, based on his changing needs, while allowing for progression toward a goal. The entire process of spiritual growth is dynamic and fluid, requiring critical, strategic thinking and constant dependence on the Spirit to reveal helpful ways to encourage and gradually build faith. The complexities of our human nature and the dynamics of the Christian life require such strategic maneuvering. The alternatives to a flexible progression that allows room to address unique needs are to either abandon flexibility for a one-size-fits-all program, or to abandon progressive goals for a method that attempts to meet whatever needs seem most urgent at the time. (For more information about designing and implementing this process see *Disciple Building: Life Coaching*, WDA.)

The R-CAPS framework is straightforward and simple to comprehend, and yet not simplistic. When we understand this process, petition God for wisdom, and use the tools given us by the Spirit of God to facilitate growth, we can effectively help people grow to maturity. We accomplish this by tracking the normal progressive phases of spiritual growth and integrating these with a set of activities that a disciple builder can employ to stimulate growth. We are convinced, both theologically and experientially, that this approach is effective in disciple building and accurately represents a biblical model for growth to maturity. Admittedly, God has only revealed the "broad strokes" of this pattern. We must look to Him to fill in the details. But even this is consistent with the whole of Scripture.

HOW TO USE THE R-CAPS GRID

A copy of the R-CAPS Grid is in the Exhibits at the end of this book. Along the top of the Grid are the Roman Numerals I-V which correspond to the phases of spiritual growth: Phase I: Establishing Faith; Phase II: Laying Foundations; Phase III: Equipping For Ministry; Phase IV: Developing New Leaders; Phase V: Developing Mature Leaders. Some of these phases are broken down into Parts A and B as well. Below the Phases are terms which describe people at various levels of spiritual maturity: New Christian, Young Christian, Ministry Trainee, New Leader and Mature Leader.

Along the left side of the Grid are listed the five initiatives or activities which can be used to facilitate growth, what we have also referred to as the "means of grace." These spell out the acronym R-CAPS: Relationships, Content, Accountability, Prayer, Situations, and give the Grid its name.

- The **R** stands for **Relationships**

- The **C** for **Content**

- The **A** for **Accountability**

- The **P** for **Prayer**

- The **S** for **Situations**

As you can see, the phases listed across the top (including subdivisions), and the activities listed on the left-hand side of the page produce a grid with 40 boxes. Each box contains a word or phrase and a number. The word or phrase describes an objective that is related to a particular stage of spiritual development and to a particular type of activity. The numbers correspond to an accompanying *R-CAPS Legend* (included as Exhibit 3) that gives more detail about that specific objective.

The purpose of the *Legend* is to give the disciple builder more specific instructions regarding how to relate (R) to the disciple, what content (C) to teach, what other traits or activities we need to hold her accountable (A) for, how to pray (P) for the disciple, and what situations (S) to put her in to encourage growth. (Included in the *Legend* are special notes that elaborate and/or clarify some key points. We have limited these to keep the process manageable.)

The Grid is a helpful disciple building tool in two ways: a) If a disciple has already demonstrated consistency (or has not demonstrated consistency) in the objectives listed in the Grid for a specific phase, it indicates to the disciple builder where the disciple is in the growth process. b) As a disciple builder identifies the phase of growth the disciple is in and references the means of grace (R-CAPS) for that phase, she is able to determine appropriate strategies to help the disciple grow.

Some leaders will be able to look at the grid and creatively design their own strategies for growth using resources and structures currently available to them. Others will need more assistance. WDA offers training seminars and resources to accompany this grid.

USING THE GRID TO DESIGN A DISCIPLE BUILDING GROWTH PROJECT

All of us have become lost or disoriented in a large suburban mall. Eventually we find the mall guide. A locator map shows the floor plan with an arrow showing our current location, along with the location of all the stores. By cross-referencing these pieces of information, we are able to navigate a path to our destination. The R-CAPS Grid works in much the same way. It helps us know the "floor plan" or pattern of spiritual growth. It helps us locate where a disciple is on the pattern, and it gives us a set of specific instructions about how to get to the destination or next phase of spiritual growth.

Let's look at an example. A disciple builder must first determine where the disciple is along the phases of growth. You can determine this by carefully studying the "Accountability" row (on the R-CAPS Grid). The objectives of the "Accountability" row are evidence of the disciple's obedience, faith and teachableness; and therefore, are the best indicators of maturity.

The *Christian Growth Checklist* (available from WDA) is an even better tool to help you accomplish this task.

It is important to remember that a disciple may appear to be farther along than she really is. For example, she may have the knowledge level (Content) or the office (Situation) of a leader, but still struggle with issues that reveal she is less mature. The wise disciple builder will look at the character and conduct traits indicated in the "Accountability" row as a more accurate measure of spiritual maturity.

Let's say you have determined that one of your disciples is in Phase III—Equipping For Ministry. A primary indicator that she has reached the "Ministry Trainee" level of maturity is that she has "become ministry-minded" (as we see in the Accountability box #18 on the Grid). Now refer to 18a-d of the *Legend* (on pages 111-131 of Exhibit 3). More specifically, we observe that she has begun to take responsibility for tasks in the ministry, that she actively takes a stand for the gospel, and that she has begun to make ministry a priority.

Continuing our example, look at the column under Phase III and locate the objective listed as Mentoring (#16) (Life Coaching). This is the objective corresponding to the "Relationships" activity, (the "R" in the R-CAPS Grid). This helps you define your role as a disciple builder in the process and the type of relationship most needed to help the disciple grow. More specifically, #16a-c of the *Legend* (page 119) tells you that your disciple needs to be a part of a select, but open group; that she needs to meet regularly with a disciple builder who can help her develop specific ministry skills; and that she needs to establish casual, evangelistic relationships with non-Christians.

By referencing the specific activities in each of the other R-CAPS boxes, the disciple builder is able to develop growth projects that will help the disciple move to the next level of maturity. (For a more detailed discussion of how to design projects using the R-CAPS Grid, see *Disciple Building: Life Coaching*, WDA.)

SIMPLE, BUT NOT SIMPLISTIC

We believe this Grid is a useful framework for Christian growth. However, we do not want to give the impression that disciple building is "simple" in the sense that it can be reduced to a one-page matrix.

Disciple building for Christ was dynamic: relational training conducted in the midst of an active ministry while being opposed by human and spiritual forces. All the activities of the disciple builder (R-CAPS) need to be understood from this perspective. Life situations (S) can put stress on relationships (R) and afford opportunities to learn new truths (C) and change priorities and values (A). Biblical truth (C) often prompts changes in life situations (S) and relationships (R). Relationships (R) can create teaching opportunities (C) and accountability (A) to ensure that the information is put into practice. Changes (S/A/R) prompt us to pray and occur because of prayer (P).

The truth Christ taught His disciples often unfolded in stages as their understanding increased. Truth builds on itself. The more basic truths lead to an understanding of the more complex truths provided we put the elemental truths into practice. It takes time to internalize many of the biblical concepts. For some, it will take longer than others. Disciple building will not be "finished" until the return of Christ, but we can lay a solid foundation and help people become mature (fully trained). By following this grid-framework, spiritual leaders are able to provide a transferable model for spiritual multiplication.

Disciple building is a very complex process, not unlike raising children. Though there are patterns of human development, every child is unique. Manuals have been written trying to assist young couples in the skills of parenting. Often advice, though simple, is not very helpful. Other advice, though specific and exhaustive, may leave us confused. Our goal is to help provide a simple model that allows the disciple builder to maintain 'the big picture' while fostering individual development. But it is no substitute for the hard work and devotion that all human development requires.

We have developed a curriculum that employs five of the six disciple building situations (See Addendum B) that provide the context in which growth occurs. (See *Disciple Building: Life Coaching*, WDA.) The curriculum is designed around a small group, a mentor relationship, the activities of ministry, a classroom, and the spiritual disciplines of an individual disciple. (Only the public gathering of the community of Christians, where corporate worship and the preaching of the Word occur, is not included as an element of the current curriculum.)

THINKING LIKE A PARENT

I'll never forget the thrill of bringing our first child home from the hospital. We were so excited about having our own baby that I never stopped by the nurses' station to pick up the owner's manual. (Later,

I discovered there *was* no owner's manual!) This seemed somewhat presumptuous, but I reasoned, "How hard can this be? You feed them, clothe them, love them. So what if they leak a little at first?"

Everything was going well, until we reached the 24-month milestone. Then the bottom fell out of our household. Our cute, adorable, cuddly little toddler had turned into a demanding, irascible little thug! And it occurred almost overnight! Later I learned that this was because we had entered into a stage of human development known (not-so-affectionately) as: "The Terrible Twos."

At this point I really lamented the absence of the owner's manual. If I had only known this was going to happen, things could have been drastically different: First, I would have prepared myself emotionally for the arrival of this little tyrant. Second, I would have made plans to head off the attempted coup. I eventually learned to prepare myself and our children for the various stages of growth that occur in life. In fact, it became quite enjoyable to first figure out, and then learn to address, the ever-changing needs of each child. At times it requires special wisdom, but having an understanding of the developmental process gives us a real advantage.

In *Disciple Building: Life Coaching*, we discuss how to design growth projects for individual disciples. By using a planning tool (NGP: a tool for designing disciple building strategies) we discover where a disciple is on the journey toward maturity, and help them take the next step. This approach is organized around the concept of discovering individual **needs(N)**, setting specific **goals(G)** and then designing manageable **projects(P)** for spiritual development. By utilizing this tool and following the progressive model outlined in the R-CAPS Grid, a disciple builder should be well on the way toward helping people grow to maturity in Christ.

But even as we affirm that disciple building can be intentional and practical, following broad patterns of spiritual development arranged around a framework modeled by Christ Himself, we must also remember that the entire process can also be confusing and unpredictable. The wise disciple builder can and should prepare.

But part of the preparation involves being ready for unexpected developments, initiatives of a good (but often mysterious), sovereign God. This will require balanced thinking supported by biblical principles and faith.

Chapter 9
Balance Is Required

BALANCING DIVINE INITIATIVE AND
HUMAN RESPONSIBILITY

Balance is required between trusting the sovereign work of the Spirit to complete the work of sanctification and relying on human efforts for spiritual growth. Biblically, it is clear that the Spirit is the facilitator and sustainer of our spiritual development. But it is clear that we too have a responsibility (Philippians 2:12-13; Colossians 1:28-29).

The Spirit of God is the One who is at work in us, both to will and work for His good pleasure. But we are admonished to work ourselves, putting into practice what the Scripture commands. As we are obedient to the Word, our character and conduct are changed. Putting truth into practice calls for diligence and discipline. This requires a plan.

Some insist that spiritual growth is exclusively a work of sovereign initiative. They say, "The Spirit is like the wind, blowing mysteriously. We cannot predict what God is going to do in our lives." There is indeed an element of truth here. Who can instruct the Lord or completely figure out His designs? Any attempt to map out a strategy to assist the Spirit in the process of our sanctification should certainly allow for God's sovereign will to prevail.

Scripture indicates that though God is the prime initiator and source of spiritual growth, we need to actively cooperate and follow the patterns He has established to govern this growth. Even the agricultural metaphor, so often used in Scripture, suggests times and seasons for planting, watering and fertilizing that allow a farmer to plan his activities. We can trust God, and we can plan (I Corinthians 3:6-8).

BALANCING POSITIONAL AND EXPERIENTIAL TRUTH

Some Scriptures describe the work of God in us as already having been completed or fulfilled. In other places, that same work is described as ongoing, incomplete and needing to be put into practice in our daily experience. For example, we already are set free from sin, and yet sin still has a grip on us that we must make an effort to overcome (Romans 6:6,12). We are saints, chosen ones, already made perfect in Christ with God Himself living and working in us. Yet we are also urged to "work out" this salvation that we already have received (Philippians 2:12). We are children of God now, but we still are being purified for a future time when we will be fully like Him (I John 3:2-3; Hebrews 10:14).

Theologians sometimes refer to this dichotomy as the difference between "positional truth" (related to our standing or position before God which is secured by Christ's death and resurrection for us) and "experiential truth" (truth we put into practice in our everyday experience). Disciple building helps integrate these two aspects of our spiritual life into a whole. We are fully accepted and loved unconditionally by God through Christ. We must teach this without compromise. But we need spiritual discipline and accountability to fully actuate that love and grace in our experience. Both are important. A focus on positional truth without an emphasis on experiential truth can produce an inconsistent walk and an unfruitful life for Christ. A focus on experiential truth without a solid foundation of positional truth can lead to legalism or negativism. Biblical disciple building helps keep the balance.

BALANCING WORLD EVANGELIZATION AND DISCIPLE BUILDING

The Twentieth Century was a period in church history characterized by unprecedented evangelism and expansion. Hopefully, this trend toward world evangelization will not abate. Many are hopeful that a corresponding emphasis on disciple building will characterize the Twenty-first Century and continue until the Return of Christ. Scripture affirms that Christ will return to a Bride who is holy and spotless, who has prepared herself for her Husband. Certainly a church who is prepared and waiting for the King will be a church that has experienced revival and restoration. This will require new organizational models that facilitate ongoing renewal. (See Addendum D.)

Jesus stated that when a disciple is fully taught he will be like his teacher (Luke 6:40). This characterization links disciple building training to the development of Christlike character and conduct. It is more than the impartation of information about Jesus and His Kingdom. It is also more than programs that involve Christians in the life of a local church. These are both vital activities and central to our work as Christians. But unless our disciple building strategies include the development of Christlike character they fall short of a biblical model. After washing the feet of His disciples, Jesus stressed that as we follow His example and obey His commands to love one another, our prayers become powerful, our joy becomes full, our likeness to Him increases, and our witness is multiplied.

In recent generations, the zeal for evangelism has increased, but our credibility as the people of God has decreased. The goal of becoming like Christ has been de-emphasized. As stewards of the gospel, we must reclaim this part of our spiritual heritage. We must, as Paul insisted, "present every man complete [mature] in Christ." (Colossians 1:28, NASB) This is also the emphasis of the Great Commission where our Lord stresses the imperative of world evangelization and church planting, but includes the importance of obeying all of His teachings. Unless we are helping Christians grow to the point where they are putting all of Christ's teachings into practice, we cannot claim to be completely fulfilling the Great Commission. Though making and baptizing disciples from all the nations is of vital importance, we must also train them to put all the truths of the Kingdom into practice. This requires much wisdom and effort, but we must do it!

BALANCING DIFFERENT SETTINGS AND STRUCTURES FOR GROWTH

Some people insist that disciple building is best achieved through "one-to-one" relationships. For others, the best disciple building environment is the small group. The worship and teaching of the public assembly is the preference of others as the best place for growth to occur. Some leaders cite the advantages of an active ministry and still others extol the personal spiritual disciplines as the best approach for spiritual formation. Actually, all of these settings were used by Jesus, and all are helpful in promoting growth.

Our Lord trained His disciples in the setting of a larger ministry to the multitudes. The admonition to "follow" and become "fishers of men" (Matthew 4:19) would have meant little if Jesus hadn't been on His way to the crowds of Galilee. Most of His teaching and training was conducted against the backdrop of the larger ministry. (In WDA, we often refer to this dynamic as "building disciples in the midst of a movement.") Though Jesus gave truth to crowds and was genuinely concerned for their welfare, He was careful to explain the applications to His small group. On some occasions, He applied truth very specifically to one or two individuals.

The Scriptures speak of growth to maturity as something the entire Christian community should aim for and also as a goal to be achieved with individual Christians (Colossians 1:28-29; Ephesians 4:11-13). To achieve this balance, disciple builders must incorporate all of the structures of the local church into their approaches and programs. (For more, see Addendum B.)

BALANCING DISCIPLE BUILDING AND LEADERSHIP

Sometimes the disciple building process in Scripture refers to equipping people for leadership roles in the church. Paul seemed to have this in mind when he admonished Timothy to entrust the "pattern of sound teaching" to faithful men who were able to transfer this truth to another generation of Christians (II Timothy 1:11-2:2). In other places, the Scriptures refer to church leaders as elders, spiritual shepherds or overseers entrusted with the care and nurture of others (I Peter 5:1-3). But growth to maturity is also for every Christian, not just the appointed leaders of the church. The Scripture clearly states that we should be equally zealous to see that every person is equipped (Colossians 1:28-29). Actually, building disciples should include both equipping leaders and assisting Christians who are not yet ready for a leadership role.

Leadership in the church is somewhat different from leadership in other settings. It is not that "up-front skills" (charisma, communication, commanding presence, etc.) are not important in the church. In fact, these abilities (along with other gifts) are often used by God when He calls people to leadership roles. But the defining qualities for leaders in the church are character-driven, an outcome of building mature disciples (I Timothy 3:1-13; Titus 1:5-9). Younger Christians should not be appointed to leadership roles, regardless of their leadership ability, until they are mature enough spiritually for the challenge (I Timothy 3:6,10). On the other hand, mature Christians who may not possess natural leadership ability, can function very effectively in some leadership roles.

Our disciple building must allow for the gradual development of leaders. This was the approach used by Jesus. At the right time, appointment to leadership is a critical component for further spiritual development. Growth occurs when Christians trust and obey God and assume responsibility for others. This leadership responsibility does not have to be an official church office. It may be simply the casual, but definite role of a faithful friend working hard to encourage others.

BALANCING LEADERSHIP DEVELOPMENT AND EMOTIONAL HEALING

As WDA developed disciple building ministries, we noticed that there were some Christians who wanted to grow spiritually but had serious trouble progressing. They faced internal obstacles. Some people got "stuck" and couldn't develop further, unable to move beyond their initial faith experience. Others went forward for awhile, and then regressed. Many eventually made progress, but only with great effort and limited success.

43

We all know Christians who may have initially progressed well in their faith, but then stopped growing, or entered a cycle of spiritual fervor followed by periods of indifference or rebellion. A primary reason for this arises from unaddressed issues of the past (often occurring in childhood) that produced coping mechanisms and/or sin-strategies. These may have enabled a person to endure and even survive childhood tragedies, but they often hinder healthy emotional and relational development in adult life. This has the effect of short-circuiting spiritual growth. Disciple builders must understand this dynamic and be able to devise strategies for helping people recover and continue to grow.

Everyone struggles at times, but some disciples seem to encounter overwhelming obstacles along the way. After repeatedly encountering this phenomenon, (and actually seeing the incidence rate increase with each subsequent year of family disintegration in Western culture) we began to ask the obvious: "Where did these obstacles come from, and how could we remove them and help people begin to grow again?"

We began to understand that though the obstacles themselves varied, they all seemed to have two similar, and often related, sources. They resulted from [1] unprocessed past pain or from [2] undeveloped emotional/relational skills and abilities that should have been formed during childhood (See *How Emotional Problems Develop*, WDA). We also began to realize that before we could help remove the obstacle(s), we had to first address the source of the obstacle(s). For this to occur, emotional and relational restoration had to also occur.

It became clear to us that effective disciple building must include restoration from the effects of these unresolved or unaddressed issues from our past. It also seemed true that Christ must have been concerned about these issues as well. As we studied this matter in the Gospels, we were encouraged to find that Christ had a built-in restorative process in His ministry.

Jesus developed mature followers who were also trained to lead His church. These were the men who "turned the world upside down." (Acts 17:6, RSV) The contemporary church needs such leaders. But

Christ's ministry involved more than leadership development. It also included helping people heal from the damages of sin. Both elements, equipping people for strategic leadership and enabling them to be restored from emotional and relational damage, must be part of an effective disciple building approach. People are restored best when they are given progressive ministry responsibility even as they address their sin issues. Such Christians, honest about their struggles but committed to becoming godly, make the best leaders.

Jesus' ministry had two related, but distinct, dimensions. One centers on our need to be restored from the destructive effects of sin. The second has to do with preparing us as citizens of His Kingdom. Both encapsulate biblical disciple building, and therefore, both are important. The first dimension is underscored by the healing and deliverance ministries of Christ. After reading the scroll of Isaiah, Jesus proclaimed His Messianic office by referring to the restorative nature of the Kingdom. (See *How Emotional Problems Develop*, WDA.) The second dimension can be seen in Christ's training, equipping and commissioning of those who followed Him. We explored this dimension earlier. (For more on the restorative dynamic in disciple building, see Addendum C.)

Chapter 10
Where Do We Go From Here?

We have considered a biblical strategy for helping Christians grow to maturity. Maturity means becoming increasingly conformed to the likeness of Jesus Christ. It's a progressive process that helps people obey the truths of Scripture and increase their understanding of God and His Kingdom. As Christians mature, they gradually change their conduct, belief systems, worldview, and ultimately, their character. Maturity also produces an increased capacity for deepening our relationship with God and others. The ultimate characteristic of maturity is sacrificial love (agape).

Jesus had a plan for helping His disciples grow to maturity. The process of disciple building is central to His Commission to the church; and therefore, it is a priority for Christian leaders. The modern church needs to rethink how we will accomplish this task. We can look to our Lord's pattern of building disciples. This approach can be compressed into a framework for ease of understanding and use, but we must balance all the dynamics that affect progressive growth.

WDA is developing a curriculum that helps leaders who want to help others grow progressively. For more information on these materials visit: www.disciplebuilding.org and download samples, order resources, or just learn more about the process. Blessings!

To Him who is able to keep you from falling and to present you before His glorious presence without fault and with great joy—to the only God our Savior be glory, majesty, power and authority, through Jesus Christ our Lord, before all ages, now and forevermore! Amen. (Jude 1:24-25)

Addendum A
The Five Phases of Growth

Phase I: Establishing Faith

The first step in becoming a disciple of Christ is to repent and believe. This includes leaving the old way-of-life and trusting in Christ as Savior. This event is referred to in Scripture as being "born again." (John 3) Whether a person comes to faith at age eight or age eighty-eight, he becomes a newborn "babe" in Christ the moment he repents and believes.

Jesus' ministry actually began with the ministry of John the Baptist. It was John's call to prepare the way for the Messiah (John 1:23) and to identify Him to His people (John 1:29). John prepared the way for Jesus by preaching the gospel (Luke 3:18) and calling people to come to the Messiah through repentance and faith. He exhorted them to be baptized as a sign of their repentance. John's ministry was quite effective. We are told that all of Israel went out to hear him (Matthew 3:5).

As John's ministry progressed, he gathered a group of disciples. This was part of the custom of the day. John's disciples were people who received his message, were baptized by him, and identified with his movement. They were with John on a regular basis and had an opportunity to hear his message on many occasions.

John's message was composed of various components of the gospel message, including the following themes or emphases:

1. Repentance and the fruits of repentance

2. Faith in the coming of the Messiah

3. Baptism

4. The Holy Spirit

5. Judgment

These components communicated the gospel message of repentance and faith and also provided immediate follow-up for those who had already believed. As the themes were repeated they reinforced the initial truth. Interestingly, Hebrews 6:1-2 lists six elementary teachings that must be understood as part of an initial foundation before Christians are able to move on to maturity in Christ.

Therefore let us leave the elementary teachings about Christ and go on to maturity, not laying again the foundation of repentance from acts that lead to death, and of faith in God, instructions about baptisms, the laying on of hands, the resurrection of the dead, and eternal judgment.

There is an amazing correspondence between the themes John emphasized and "the elementary teachings" of Hebrews 6:1-2. (The "laying on of hands" is probably a reference to a practice in the early church of laying hands on a person at their baptism as a symbol of having received the Holy Spirit.) There is a need to provide an opportunity for all new Christians to review and gain a more complete understanding of the components of the gospel. This serves as a starting point for their Christian growth.

John's ministry provided the initial evangelistic thrust that helped to launch Christ's ministry. (Jesus' first disciples were initially followers of John.) John preached for about six months before Christ started His ministry. Afterward, John's ministry continued as a parallel ministry of evangelism until his arrest and execution.

Phase II: Laying Foundations

The focus of this next phase in the life of the Christian is on gaining a better understanding of who Christ is and how to follow Him. As the new Christian learns more of Christ's nature and character, she learns to trust Him not only for salvation, but for other things as well. During this phase, Jesus invited His disciples to spend more time with Him so that He could reveal Himself more fully to them. Jesus invited a few of John's disciples to be His followers. John had singled Christ out to his disciples as the "Lamb of God." (John 1:35-41) These initial disciples found some others, and Jesus also found others. In this way He quickly developed a small band of His own disciples. The ministry of Christ didn't become very large during this phase. Noting this, some theologians refer to this phase of ministry as the "year of obscurity." Actually, it only lasted about 6-9 months, and was characterized by Jesus essentially leading a small group.

Jesus' primary emphasis during this period was to reveal Himself to His followers and build a relationship with them. So He kept His ministry small and spent a lot of time with them. During this period these early disciples became convinced that they had found the Messiah (John 1:35-51). They had not yet left their jobs to travel with Him, but He did take them on a couple of journeys.

Few people have a very comprehensive view of who Christ is when they first trust Him. They come simply hoping that He will make a difference in their life, often out of a sense of desperation. One of the first things that people need is a more comprehensive picture of who Jesus Christ is. This is exactly what Jesus did for His first followers. He revealed Himself to them by making claims about Himself, doing Messianic works, and confirming these claims through two significant miracles.

Young Christians today need the same things. They need to gather in small groups and learn about who Jesus is, how to build a relationship with Him, and how to begin to follow Him. They need to see God answer their prayers and start to meet their needs. They need a leader who will model the Christian life before them and build a relationship with them. These small groups become focal points of a new spiritual family, a place where many needs are met.

JESUS PROVIDES THE EXAMPLE

Jesus modeled many aspects of the Christian life for His disciples during this phase of ministry. He modeled spending time with the

Father and walking in dependence upon the Father. He also modeled what He would ask His followers to do next. Actually, Jesus did this throughout His ministry, never challenging them to do anything that they had not seen Him do first.

Anticipating the period of outreach and evangelism training that was coming, He modeled this, offering salvation to those in need. He reached out to the religious leaders when He told Nicodemus he needed to be born again (John 3:1-8). He reached out to the downtrodden when He offered living water to the woman at the well (John 4:1-26). And He offered salvation to many others who felt ostracized by the religious establishment as they came to Him in the desert (John 3:22).

A faithful Life Coach (or mentor) is an important key to growth at this time in a disciple's life. Since much of Christianity is learned from watching the example of others, the mentor needs to be a good role model. She needs to spend time with Christ, share Christ with others, trust Christ to meet her needs, and exhibit enthusiasm and a commitment to grow spiritually.

At this phase Jesus involved His young disciples in the ministry strategically, giving them important and necessary tasks. He had them baptize people (not a function of ordained clergy in His day), purchase and manage the food, take care of the money, provide transportation, etc. This helped assimilate them into His movement and made them feel like an important part of His Kingdom. But the tasks He assigned did not include leadership roles, or anything that could become spiritually embarrassing, over-challenging their faith.

As new Christians start developing a relationship with Christ, they see answers to prayer and experience changes in their lives. Subsequently, they get more excited about their new life of following Christ. At this time, many of them will begin to tell others about Christ. This is natural and should be encouraged as a natural outcome of their experience. Often they begin to want more of their Life Coach's time and more information that will help them grow. As we observe these developments, we should realize that they are becoming ready for the next phase of disciple building: Equipping For Ministry.

Phase III: Equipping For Ministry

In this phase, a disciple learns to serve others and engage in ministry opportunities under the guidance of more mature Christians. In the Gospels, this was when Jesus challenged some of His disciples: "Follow Me, and I will make you fishers of men." (Matthew 4:19, NASB) This call indicated that He was moving them to the next phase of growth. Once they decided to follow Him, Jesus took His disciples with Him on a mission trip where He taught and ministered to others.

Jesus launched this period of ministry by making two major changes. Up until now His ministry had been mostly private, occurring in remote areas. But at this time, Jesus shifted His ministry to the public arena. He did this by healing many people and casting out demons (which tended to draw some attention; cf. Luke 4:31-44). Crowds followed Him and the movement quickly expanded. As interest grew, Jesus also began His public teaching ministry. The first change is a shift from private ministry to public ministry. This dynamic continued until the very end.

FISHERS OF MEN

The second change in Jesus' ministry involved challenging His disciples to become "fishers of men." (Matthew 4:19) This seemed to include most of His early followers. Later He added Matthew, and He may have added others also. (It is not clear how many people He challenged in this way, but by the end of this phase it probably included all of those He would later appoint as apostles.)

Jesus took His men on a series of evangelistic tours. His method of training at this point was fairly simple: He included the disciples in His evangelistic ministry. Because of the public miracles, He was attracting a large, interested crowd. Obviously, not everyone was able to get very close to Jesus. This growing public ministry created many private opportunities for His disciples to share their faith, explaining who Jesus was and what He had done for them.

In the same way, we need to individually challenge those who are ready to join a ministry training group. We need to train them how to present the gospel, share their testimonies, and relate to non-Christians. We need to provide opportunities for them to share the gospel with those who are interested in knowing more about Jesus.

Jesus' method of teaching in this period of time was to place His disciples in situations where they would be forced to sort out issues related to legalism and the freedom they enjoyed in their relationship to Him. He did this by creating several Sabbath controversies. One of His favorite activities involved healing someone on the Sabbath, thus creating a debate about the Sabbath laws. This provided a forum to teach about who He was and to expose the legalism and inadequacy of the Jewish leadership. It also created an opportunity for Him to teach healthy perspectives on ministry and freedom in the Christian walk.

The teaching in this phase came as an outgrowth of Christ's evangelistic ministry. Through repeated presentations of the gospel, Jesus' disciples heard more and more about the benefits of the gospel. In addition, they were confronted with difficulties and opposition that presented other opportunities to learn. As our disciples become involved in sharing the gospel, they too will grow in their appreciation of what Christ has done for them; and they too will run into problems as they meet people with differing beliefs. This will create other opportunities to clarify truth.

Jesus modeled mature leadership by showing compassion for hurting people, making the most of the natural opportunities for ministry that came His way every day, teaching with authority, proclaiming the gospel boldly, continuing to reach out to new people, and demonstrating His power over demons. He involved His disciples in many of these activities during the Phase III experience and modeled others in anticipation of Phase IV.

A NEW IDENTITY

Phase III is an important period for helping people understand their new identity as Christians. As The Twelve served alongside Jesus as "fishers of men," the experience helped them better understand their new role and position in the Kingdom. The instruction Jesus gave regarding law and grace also clarifies the Christian's identity in Christ. (Interestingly, this same approach is used by Paul in the Epistles.)

A new relationship with God begins when someone believes in Christ as Lord and Savior, trusting that He died for sins, reconciling them to God. Scripture affirms that when this occurs someone is "born again" through His Spirit and receives a new identity as a child of God (John 3:3-8; Romans 8:12-16; II Corinthians 5:17-18a). But, in addition to being accepted in Christ, Christians are also invited to participate with God in building and extending His Kingdom (II Corinthians 5:18b-20). This "ministry of reconciliation" serves to further clarify our new identity in Christ (viz.): royal children who serve as royal ambassadors.

In one sense, God doesn't need us to accomplish His plans and purposes; He is, after all, Almighty God. But, (amazingly!), He calls and invites us to minister alongside Him, thus tactically linking the success of His mission on earth to our participation (Romans 10:14-15). Sharing the gospel is a catalyst for even further understanding (Philemon 6). As we realize that God's plan for extending His Kingdom includes this strategic role for us, it provides great hope and encouragement. We, who once were enemies of God, are now His children, allies, and partners; we are citizens and servants of heaven, emissaries of an Eternal King.

Phases II and III are where we lay the foundation for Christian growth and equip people for ministry. But not everyone challenged for ministry training progresses immediately to leadership. Phase III also serves as a filter for selecting future leaders, and helps determine their pace and degree of involvement. (See *Disciple Building: Life Coaching*, WDA for a more detailed discussion of filters and pacing.)

Phase IV: Developing New Leaders

When a Christian progresses to this phase, she is ready to take responsibility for the spiritual well-being of others. During this period Jesus taught His disciples how to live in His Kingdom. In addition,

He appointed The Twelve to be apostles and sent them out on their own to preach the Kingdom of God and to minister to people's needs. Mark 3:14-15 summarizes what Jesus did during this phase.

He appointed twelve [designating them apostles] that they might be with Him and that He might send them out to preach and to have authority to drive out demons.

This phase actually has two parts to it. The first part involves appointing and instructing His new leadership in Kingdom principles. The second part involves Christ creating a series of situations that forced His leaders to reevaluate their expectations of what it means to follow Him. This reevaluation crisis is pivotal, centering on whether or not leaders choose the eternal benefits of following Christ, or opt for leadership roles that allow them temporal power and success.

APPOINTING THE TWELVE

As Jesus begins this new phase in His ministry, He prays all night (Luke 6:12). This is an unusual occurrence in His ministry but signals that something very important is about to happen. After calling all of His disciples together He appointed The Twelve as apostles. They formed the core of His leadership team. It is clear that Jesus was preparing them for their future ministry assignment, when He would send them into all the world. (The word "apostle" actually means "sent one or missionary.")

Jesus' appointment of The Twelve was the beginning point of a two-year training process designed to prepare them for the time that He would leave them in charge of the church. Interestingly, rather than send them out at this point to have their own ministry, He draws them even closer and spends more time teaching them and being with them. This is an important point for modern disciple builders. Throughout the ministry, Jesus gradually required more and more from His disciples, both time and commitment. In turn, He also gave them more of His time and focused attention. Our tendency in the modern church is to give developing leaders more responsibility, but not more time. We would be wise to follow Christ's example and spend significant amounts of time building relationships with and developing these new leaders.

In Phase IV Jesus sent The Twelve out to preach and gave them authority to cast out demons (Luke 9:1-9). Jesus began doing these activities in Phase III. And having modeled them in Phase III, He now gave The Twelve the same responsibilities in Phase IV. As we have already observed, Jesus always modeled the activities He would give His disciples before He asked them to do the activities.

The word translated "preach" has a wide range of meanings: from preaching the gospel to teaching dogma. In this setting it seems to indicate that The Twelve now had the responsibility and privilege to expand the preaching and teaching that Jesus did. For the first time, they shared the preaching duties with Him, proclaiming His Kingdom and exercising His authority. This delegation of responsibility and authority is profound. The apostles would continue this until they each died. It even extended into the writing and compilation of the New Testament Scriptures.

PUTTING ON SPIRITUAL ARMOR

In this Phase, Jesus also gave them authority to cast out demons and heal the sick. Before sending them out (cf. Luke 9:1-2/Mark 3:14-15), He gave a great deal of instruction and some additional modelling regarding how to conduct spiritual warfare. By teaching the Parables of the Kingdom, He also instructed them further on the type of warfare they would face. Spiritual warfare in the modern church is an area often characterized by extremes. It seems we either focus too much attention on the evil one and his schemes, or not enough. Jesus provided a balanced approach. He progressively trained His disciples in the area of spiritual warfare. The disciple building instruction and experiences of Phases II through the first half of Phase IV represent what Paul referred to as putting on of the "armor of God." (Ephesians 6:10-18)

In Phase II, Jesus' disciples learned that they could be confident that Christ was their Savior and King: the equivalent of putting on the "helmet of salvation." In Phase III, Jesus modeled spiritual warfare by casting many demons out of many people on many occasions, demonstrating His authority over all His creation, including Satan and his demonic forces. He also trained His disciples in evangelism, in essence fitting their feet with the readiness of the "gospel of peace." Also in Phase III, much of the teaching focused on their position in Christ. This concept is directly related to putting on the "breastplate of righteousness."

Throughout the first three phases and into Phase IV, the disciples were taught a variety of foundational truths needed to resist and defeat the Devil. Jesus understood that the Christian life was difficult. The weapons-of-choice for the evil one are lies, wayward thoughts, suggestions, subtle accusations, etc. The battles are fought close-at-hand, occurring in areas where we are most vulnerable because of past pain, and affecting our closest relationships. This hand-to-hand combat requires both the "sword of the Spirit" and the "shield of faith." The truths of the Word give us the ability to rebuke the evil one for his lies, while simultaneously enabling us to persevere, resisting the roaring lion, trusting God.

Once the spiritual warfare training was completed, Jesus sent them out with authority to cast out demons. He also modeled how to pray for protection from the evil one (cf. John 17/Ephesians 6:18-20). All of these weapons are required to protect us against the counter-attacks of Satan as we move into his territory and take back what he has controlled. Jesus knew this. He gave His disciples the weapons they needed and gives us the same armor.

THE SERMON ON THE MOUNT

As already stated, during this period Jesus spent a lot of time teaching His disciples. In the first part of Phase IV, He taught primarily about the Kingdom of God in two major sections of Scripture: the Sermon on the Mount and the Parables of the Kingdom. The Sermon on the Mount is considered Christ's most important and central set of instructions, the highlight of all that He taught. In the Sermon, He sets forth the standards for those who would be a part of the Kingdom of God and who would lead in His Kingdom. It unveiled Christ as the Old Testament Law-Giver (God Himself) and clarified how the Law integrates with His New Covenant/Testament (a work of grace which occurs first in the heart and gradually works outward to affect all of life). In addition, His teaching in the Sermon helped prepare His disciples (who were Jews) for their role as leaders of the church among the Gentile nations.

It is important to understand that Jesus did not introduce the concept of law (standards of righteousness) to His disciples until after He had been with them for some time. (Unlike the Pharisees who built their entire ministry on the Law.) Instead, He initially built a solid relationship of unconditional love with them in Phase II. Then in Phase III, He emphasized grace as the ongoing basis of His relationship with them. It is not until Phase IV that He introduces the concept of law.

When we understand that Christianity is primarily a relationship with Christ (and not a set of rules to follow), and that our relationship with Christ is based on grace (and not based on following a set of rules), then we are able to consider, "How can I best please God?" At this point in the maturation process, we begin to see the benefits of being conformed to the likeness of Christ the King. As King and Law-Giver, He wants us to live according to His Kingdom principles, revealed primarily in The Sermon on the Mount. These principles of righteous living (law) then become a way for us to please God, because we want to, not requirements we must fulfill in order to be accepted by Him. The law thus finds a proper place in the Christian's life. It gives wisdom and guidance to those who want to please God, a fitting response to the love and grace God has shown to them.

PROGRESSIVE EVANGELISM TRAINING

About half way through this Phase, Jesus sent The Twelve out in pairs to do evangelism. He sent them into villages ahead of Him with specific instructions: take no money and stay in the places where the gospel was welcomed. This approach, which requires a lot of faith, is often taught by modern trainers as the best form of evangelism. But we must remember that Jesus taught evangelism progressively.

In Phase III His initial miracles and teaching created interest and curiosity, a relatively non-threatening environment where His disciples could entertain questions about Him from the crowd of onlookers, and share their personal experience. After they became accustomed to sharing their faith in this way, Jesus prepared them for more difficult situations.

Then in Phase IV, He sent them out in pairs without Him. Later, He took them into Gentile regions and exposed them to cross-cultural evangelism. Jesus gradually moved from less-threatening forms of evangelism to more difficult and diverse forms of evangelism. At the end of His ministry Jesus commissioned His disciples to take the gospel to the whole world.

TIME OF RE-EVALUATION

In the second half of Phase IV Jesus put His leaders in situations where they were forced to reevaluate their expectations of Christianity. Up until then, the ministry had been generally well-accepted by the crowds with little resistance and growing popularity. It was considered beneficial to be associated with Jesus. But all this was about to change.

We are told in John 6 that the crowds wanted to make Jesus their king. But Jesus didn't come to be the kind of king they wanted. So He preached a very difficult sermon designed to reject their offer of kingship and expose their wrong motives for wanting to make Him king (John 6:25-59). The result was that many of His disciples stopped walking with Him (John 6:60-66). It appears that He intentionally purged His ministry. The most committed remained with Him, but even they were confused (John 6:67-69). This situation increased opposition to His Kingdom, setting the stage for The Twelve to re-evaluate their priorities.

We must understand that, instead of avoiding a clash of values and worldviews, Jesus actually precipitated this crisis. Modern disciple builders should expect nothing less. The Spirit will create various situations that cause the disciples we train to want to leave the ministry. We need to encourage them, but avoid trying to circumvent this painful, but necessary, experience.

During this Phase, Jesus began to challenge the religious establishment much more strongly, exposing hypocrisy and wrong motives. It became clear for the first time that Jesus was not trying to reform Judaism. He was actually starting an entirely new movement, the church. The reaction of the Jewish leaders became more hostile to Jesus and they began to develop a plan to kill Him (John 7:1). (For the most part He avoided dangerous places, especially Jerusalem. He even made a trip into the Gentile regions of Tyre and Sidon (Mark 7:24-8:10) where it was somewhat safe.)

By the second half of Phase IV, it was becoming clear that living perfectly by the Sermon on the Mount was not possible. His initial call to inner heart-righteousness probably motivated His disciples to live accordingly. But it eventually became clear that they fell far short of that standard. The law tends to affect all Christians in this way, motivating us to compliance at first, but discouraging us later as we realize that we are unable to keep it faithfully. This causes us to either adapt the law, changing it to conform to our abilities and preferences; or to fall back on the true basis for our acceptance by God: (viz.) grace working through faith.

All of the different events that occurred in the second part of Phase IV created a crisis for Jesus' disciples. It was a difficult time. They struggled with the call to follow Him. These latest developments were not what they expected. Things were very different now, and they were forced to re-think everything they had been taught growing up in Judaism, and what it meant to follow the Messiah. They were forced to drastically change their worldview, which had become too temporal and short-sighted. Their faith was stretched at every point. Phase IV is a time of great tension and personal struggle, a time of crisis and catharsis.

STRUCTURING GROWTH

Sometimes we can structure the circumstances that are needed for disciples to grow. Often we can't. As leaders, we too have to trust God. Looking to God to create the circumstances for growth to occur builds our faith as disciple builders. Sometimes we need encouraging things to happen, and sometimes we need challenging, faith-stretching events to occur. God sovereignly provided many of the situations that caused the first disciples to grow. Jesus' human leadership created many of the specific situations, but the Father was the Architect of the overall application.

There is always a balance between what we do and what God does. If God does not do His part, we will never complete the task. But He will. He has called us to make disciples and He has made His authority available to achieve His purposes. In Phase IV, our disciples need to go through a crisis of faith. God will bring it about. Be prepared for it.

Phase V: Developing Mature Leaders

In this final phase of the training, Jesus gave His disciples increasing responsibilities for leadership. In addition, He instructed them regarding the priority of servant-leadership. They were to love and serve each other even if it meant sacrificing their lives. Ultimately He commissioned them to go to the whole world with the good news, discipling others in the same way they had been equipped.

This phase also has two parts to it. The first part is focused on developing the overall ministry of the entire community of Christians. The second part is yet another difficult time for Jesus' disciples. Ironically, their effective ministry and leadership caused their pride to emerge. They needed to be reminded again that they were incapable, in their own strength, of fulfilling their call and mission. It was only in His strength, carried out through the person of the Holy Spirit, that they would be able to live the Christian life.

JESUS REPEATS HIS TEACHING

In this phase, Jesus appointed a second group of leaders, The Seventy (Luke 10:1). As we observed earlier, these new leaders were just entering Phase IV, training just completed by The Twelve. We should expect Jesus to repeat the Phase IV themes with this second group. And this is exactly what we find in the Gospel account. All the major themes of Phase IV are repeated in Phase V, obviously for this new group of leaders.

But there is also a whole new set of instructions given for the benefit of The Twelve. The fact that Jesus repeated what He did in Phase IV for The Seventy is tremendously significant. It means that He saw what He was doing as a repeatable pattern. This is most likely the pattern Paul mentioned to Timothy (II Timothy 1:13-2:2) and is the same pattern that we need to follow today. It is also clear that Jesus intended to multiply His leadership. In order for that to happen there would have to be multiple phases of growth occurring simultaneously. It is obvious that this occurred, there is no other reasonable explanation for the emergence of The Seventy.

RELATIONSHIPS CHANGE

As we mentioned earlier, Jesus spent more and more time with His leaders after He appointed them. But in Phase V, Jesus began to lessen His involvement with The Twelve. Undoubtedly the ministry became larger with the addition of new leaders. Jesus needed help equipping The Seventy. This required delegating additional responsibilities to The Twelve and probably involved changes for Jesus also. The result was less interaction between Jesus and The Twelve.

Rather than being detrimental to their development, this situation is just what The Twelve needed to begin to establish their own independent ministries, an event that is crucial if multiplication is to occur. A large movement can become unwieldy if there are not enough middle leaders in place. But when disciple builders conduct the training of Phases IV and V effectively, there should be adequate leaders for future expansion.

Helping Jesus with The Seventy was a new assignment for The Twelve who progressively advanced in their leadership roles. One of the big factors in their spiritual development occurred as Jesus gradually increased their ministry opportunities and responsibilities during each new Phase of growth. Jesus began the equipping of His ministry leaders in Phase III and the training continued until He left this world at the end of Phase V. At that time His ministry was placed fully in the hands of the leaders He developed. They continued to grow and be challenged (as the book of Acts testifies) but He had fully trained them for their leadership roles in the church. We can and must accomplish this same training today.

RELATIONAL DYNAMICS

In the first part of Phase V, Jesus taught many new principles regarding how the body of Christ should function. Much of Christ's teaching in this phase came in response to questions brought up by The Twelve. They needed to know how to handle different problems they had encountered as they related to others involved in the ministry. Their leadership responsibilities created situations that challenged their abilities and authority. Jesus used this situation as a teaching opportunity. In fact, most of the principles of servant-leadership can only be fully understood when leaders grapple with real-life situations.

Reading books and attending seminars are helpful, but only to a point. Relational pressures and spiritual warfare are the crucible for real leadership development. Leaders at Phase V should be given responsible leadership roles. They should help younger leaders and develop ministries based on their spiritual gifts and calling (cf. Ephesians 4:11-16).

PRIDE AND LEADERSHIP

Sometimes it's easy to envision The Twelve as bumbling and ineffective while they were with Jesus. We tend to think of Christ as the Master, and The Twelve as more like Abbot and Costello, or the Three Stooges. While it is true they made mistakes and often held wrong perspectives, they also dispatched successful ministries. They had done everything asked of them. Their training was nearly complete. Because they had successfully completed the equipping process and had risen to leadership roles alongside of Jesus, they began to argue among themselves about who was the greatest. Two felt they deserved cabinet positions in the coming Kingdom, prompting indignant responses from the others, and one was rebuked as a mouthpiece of Satan. Their effectiveness revealed a hidden weakness: spiritual pride.

Does this sound familiar? It should. I have lost track of all the times I have been involved in ego-wars with others in leadership. We should not be surprised at this development, but we need to be aware of the dynamics behind this situation. The church desperately needs mature leaders, men and women who are willing to have the same attitude as Christ, considering others more important than themselves (Philippians 2:1-16). But the evil one wants to divide us, knowing that a "household divided against itself will not stand." (Matthew 12:25)

We must begin by admitting that indwelling sin is the root cause for arguments among Christians. James makes the point clearly (James 3:13-4:3). We argue because we are self-seeking. The answer is simple: we need to die to self and live for Christ and others. By doing so we are raised up by Him and given the honor we desire, but in His time frame, not ours.

If this were the only cause of relational struggle, the solution might be simple: find the sinful party(ies), and exhort them to repent. But it is often more complicated. When we do something new in the Christian life, we tend to rely heavily upon Christ for strength, wisdom, protection, etc. But as we become experienced, we also become confident. Sometimes confidence is a good thing, inspiring courage and biblical risk-taking. Sometimes it can become ugly, causing us to become smug and self-sufficient.

When we rely on ourselves, rather than rebuke us sternly, God instead disciplines us out of love. He does this so "that we may share in his holiness."(Hebrews 12:10) We see our inability to accomplish anything without His abiding Presence, and we are also reminded of His unconditional love and acceptance. This is a good pattern that causes growth and development. This is what the writer of Hebrews had in mind when he said, "No discipline seems pleasant at the time, but painful. Later on, however, it produces a harvest of righteousness and peace for those who have been trained [discipled] by it." (Hebrews 12:11)

Another complicating factor is the role of the evil one in this process. Satan desires to "sift [us] like wheat," just like he did with Peter (Luke 22:31). The evil one is described later by Peter as "a roaring lion looking for someone to devour." (I Peter 5:8-9) Peter, who was encouraged by Jesus to strengthen his brothers after he had repented of his own pride, warns us to "resist him [the evil one], standing firm in the faith, because you know that your brothers throughout the world are undergoing the same kind of sufferings." Peter learned this from being with Jesus.

GREATER DEPENDENCE ON GOD

This pattern is repeated throughout the Christian life at all phases of development. God calls us to a difficult task and provides the grace to accomplish it. As we become self-confident, He allows events designed to humble us. Sometimes, God even allows the enemy to attack us (Luke 22:24-32).

In the second part of Phase V Jesus taught about His Second Coming even as He prepared them for His leaving. More importantly, He died. This event totally disoriented them. In spite of the realignment of their expectations (this began to occur in Phase IV), the disciples continued to hold on to unrealistic perspectives of what His life (and theirs!) would be like while He was on earth. They still hoped for prominent roles among God's religious elite. Even though He had repeatedly told them of His imminent death at the hands of the religious establishment, they didn't see it coming. Ironically, the crucifixion of Christ's body led to the crucifixion of the flesh (pride) of His disciples.

This still occurs today. Modern Christian leaders can develop expectations for how God wants to work in and through them. Sometimes these expectations may not be perfectly aligned with God's will. When things don't go as they planned or hoped, people can become disappointed and discouraged. Sometimes this leads to bitterness, with others being hurt also. (Hebrews 12:11-15) Scripture asserts that planning and hoping for specific results is not necessarily a bad development: "In his heart a man plans his course…" (Proverbs 16:9a) However, God reserves the right to determine the final outcome: "…but the Lord directs his steps." (Proverbs 16:9b) As we submit to His agenda, we gain wisdom and learn to increasingly rely on His Spirit to enable and guide us. If we harden our heart, we can become stubborn and require stricter discipline.

After Christ's crucifixion, His disciples fled and went into hiding. They were confused and frightened. Scripture doesn't tell us everything about this period, but it does reveal their abject disappointment and loss of hope. Things changed quickly once reports of Jesus' resurrection began to reach them. Once He appeared to them, they gained a new perspective, and a process of restoration, healing, and transition began to take place. Their hope returned, but it was a hope tempered by wisdom and a new dependence on the Spirit.

This entire situation was very humbling to Jesus' first disciples. They saw their weakness and need for Christ in a new light. It wasn't that they hadn't understood at all, but they had understood partially, inadequately. But after these final events of His earthly ministry, they "got it." At least some of them did. At the end (or maybe we should say at the new beginning), Jesus had fully prepared them, and He left the ministry in their hands. He gave them the Great Commission, ascended to Heaven and sent them the Holy Spirit to live in them and fill them. Then they continued the ministry that Jesus began, and spread it all over the world.

In one sense, what occurred at Jesus' death and resurrection and the events leading to Pentecost will never be repeated again. The Spirit will never be sent again by Christ, in the same way. There will never again be a Master Disciple Builder like Jesus. Never again will a group of apostles establish the church and canonize His teachings in Scripture.

But in another sense, what happened to those first disciples happens over and over again. Modern Christians follow Jesus (through His Spirit within us), and He leads us and teaches us. We become active in a community of faith, and begin to practice the spiritual disciplines. We learn doctrine and how to share our faith. Many of us become modern apostles, "sent ones" who plant ministries and assume official leadership roles. All of us assume some kind of leadership, even if it's only as examples of Jesus in our neighborhood. And as disappointments occur, we too can become jaded, or self-sufficient, or proud, and need to be reminded of who He is, and who we are, all over again. We will need to have our eyes opened again and again, until the moment we see Him face-to-face. Then we will be changed completely, perfectly conformed to His likeness (I John 3:2).

Jesus had a plan and process for helping His people grow to maturity. It involved developing leaders who were able to teach "all things whatsoever [He] commanded" to subsequent generations of Christians (Matthew 28:20, KJV). This pattern of progressive disciple building doesn't prevent struggle. But when struggles occur, sound training helps us "keep our wits about us" and provides perspective and wisdom. This disciple building experience not only equips us to grow, it also gives us a platform for helping others grow. And the process continues.

Addendum B
R-CAPS:
Five Initiatives of a Disciple Builder
R: Everything Begins with a _Relationship_

Relationships are at the heart of disciple building. Jesus was _with_ His men. He loved them, exhorted them and took them with Him. "Come and see," and "Follow me!" were invitations to discover who He was in everyday life. Modern disciples also need someone who loves them. They sometimes arrive at our door with hurt feelings and disillusionment. They may feel that no one cares enough to relate to them, help them deal with their struggles or train them to grow up in the faith. Unless people know we care they will not trust us enough to listen to what we say. We too must be _with_ people if we hope to impact their lives. This is certainly true of children.

Someone said that love for a child is spelled T-I-M-E. This is also true of spiritual children. Accountability without love will frustrate and eventually fail. Often it is not what we say, but how we live and relate that affects people the most.

Unfortunately, in our fast-paced world, relationships can be neglected. We may be tempted to think that we can influence others by simply dumping information on them. But building solid men and women of God requires establishing relationships. This takes more time and effort, but in the long run it pays greater dividends. Through caring relationships, we can appreciably impact the life of someone else.

Leaders must be wise and consistent, sacrificing in the short term to establish fruit that will remain and reproduce. An emphasis on evangelism without relational, accountable disciple building is an incomplete fulfillment of the Great Commission. It will not be easy to rectify this, but if we begin now, with this present generation, we can address deficiencies and build for the future. This will require changing our thinking and our structures.

As we explored the ministry of Jesus, we saw repeatedly that He modeled truth before He taught it. Then, He taught skills that involved Him working alongside His disciples, making sure they understood before He gave responsibilities. Next, He allowed them to undertake ministry activities without Him being present, and eventually, He left them entirely, expecting them to handle matters without Him being around at all. This process of gradually training someone by changing the nature of the relationship and our involvement in the process is called the OPSI *Steps of Transfer* (derived from an acronym for the four stages of transference):

1. Observation: They watch or observe us as we do it.

2. Participation: They participate in the activity with us.

3. Supervision: We allow them to do it, and we oversee the activity, providing feedback.

4. Independence: They accomplish the activity apart from us.

This process is used over and over in effective disciple building. Nearly every new skill requires some application of the OPSI *Steps of Transfer*. Modeling is absolutely critical for the process to work. For this reason, disciple builders must be prepared to "get in the trenches" and do the work of the ministry alongside those we are training. It is not enough to give them manuals to read. We must do ministry with them, relationally. (For more details about OPSI, see Exhibit 3, the *R-CAPS Legend*.)

But modeling is only part of the relationship. Disciples must know that we really care, that we love God and that we love them. This can't be contrived. People aren't fooled by phony love. The Scriptures exhort us, "Let love be without hypocrisy." (Romans 12:9a, NASB) People can sense when they are being used for "ministry purposes," and when someone really loves them. Only Christ can give us the ability to really love. Actually, this is the purpose-driven goal of disciple building, growth to maturity. "The goal of this command is love, which comes from a pure heart and a good conscience, and a sincere faith." (I Timothy 1:5) In another place Paul reminded his disciples, "As apostles of Christ we could have been a burden to you, but we were gentle among you, like a mother caring for her children. We loved you so much that we were delighted to share with you not only the gospel of God but our lives as well, because you had become so dear to us." (I Thessalonians 2:6b-8)

This kind of love is not natural. If we want to help others we have to grow also and become like Him, willing to lay down our lives for others. Jesus summed it up by saying, "…all men will know that you are My disciples, if you love one another." (John 13:35) "Greater love has no one than this, that one lay down his life for his friends." (John 15:13, NASB)

C: *Content* is Critical for Growth

The Scriptures testify that the Word of God is powerful, setting us free from sin, enabling us to walk uprightly before God, equipping us for every good work. Disciples need to be taught the Word of God. We must instruct them faithfully and patiently, pointing out promises, principles, the characteristics and attributes of a good God who loves them. We must instruct and train them in spiritual warfare and the skills of ministry. They need to know theology and how to understand and study the Bible, the source of theology. They need to know about mankind and the redemption of the cross. The list of the things they need to know is long and complicated. Teaching content is central to the disciple building process, because truth changes people.

But it's not truth learned in a vacuum that changes people. Growth occurs when truth does its work in us. Truth that changes must be appropriated into all of life. It is not enough to just hear a good sermon, meditate on a passage of Scripture, or read a good book. Simply holding (even tenaciously) to a theological position will not deeply affect our heart or behavior. (Some of the most unchristlike people have the best doctrine.) Truth must be obeyed if it's going to set us free or enable us to help others.

For this reason, disciple building learning projects must be designed with application in mind. This approach requires more than lectures or reading lists. We must consider the agents and structures that facilitate the "doing" of truth, and develop training, small group studies, growth projects, and theological concepts to encourage application. Driven by relationships and prayer, this curriculum needs to be built on the premise that growth occurs gradually and progressively, and that appropriate accountability must be a hallmark of the process. (Visit www.disciplebuilding.org to learn more about WDA's curriculum.)

A: _Accountability_ is not a "Dirty Word"

Jesus explicitly said to teach them "to obey everything." (Matthew 28:20) Teaching truth isn't enough (as every parent knows). We must teach truth so that a disciple will obey the truth. This requires patience, wisdom and accountability. For this to occur, we must design some type of supervisory structure and process where we can observe whether or not a disciple is doing what Christ commanded, and have in place the relational pressure points needed to encourage obedience. As a manager once said, "It's not what you expect, but what you inspect that matters." Unfortunately, we live in a day when any form of inspection is viewed as meddling or (worse) controlling. To avoid interfering in the life of a disciple, we must understand what is appropriate for that particular disciple. Wise assessment is a must. And to wisely discern, we need some type of measurement.

The youth meeting was packed with teenagers, many of whom had never darkened the door of the church prior to that night. Many of them came from the "bad part of town." They sat in the back; hard, bitter, suspicious. But the live music, entertaining speaker, and caring authenticity of the youth group had attracted them. As the message shifted from popular culture to the Christian life, you could sense the Spirit working. Some in the back came forward weeping, others shifted in their seats, nervous as they considered His life and claims. Finally, one young man bolted for the door. I recognized him as someone I had spoken to earlier as we canvassed the community inviting people to the event. I followed him into the summer night.

As I approached I could see he was struggling to understand and genuinely wanted to believe, but an abusive father and life on the streets had made him suspicious, jaded. He was angry, but willing to talk. I sensed no one had ever loved him, accepting him just as he was. As we talked about Christ and the life He offered, in an attempt to quiet jangled nerves he lit a cigarette, tacitly admitting that he felt weak, alone, confused. I was about to suggest that we pray together, asking God for answers, when one of the adult leaders assigned to open the church hall for the meeting approached. I was stunned when I heard the scathing rebuke: "Put out that cigarette right now or get off this property! We don't allow smoking here, our bodies are temples of the Holy Spirit!"

I never saw that young man again. He crushed out the cigarette as instructed, and turned away. As he left, I offered an awkward explanation, but the moment had passed. At first I was angry at the church leader. One abrupt exhortation and all of the work and prayer that had been faithfully invested to reach that young man were wasted. Later, I realized that the church leader was also trying to be faithful, holding people accountable to the Word (as he understood it). And it was not as if I liked smoking. I was no fan of the tobacco industry. This habit had recently killed my mother. But smoking wasn't the point.

Accountability, though perhaps well intended, was misplaced. Our accountability must be driven by proper assessment of needs and fueled by genuine love; by-products of relational, progressive disciple building. Dealing with the habit of smoking wasn't the primary need of that young man that night. His primary need was for love, acceptance, grace. He desperately wanted to see the kindness of God, which in turn, leads to repentance. Eventually we would have discussed smoking, but later after a solid spiritual foundation had been laid. Maybe we wouldn't have needed to discuss it at all, the Spirit often prompts young Christians to abandon old lifestyle habits.

Accountability (assessment, affirmation and recognition of needs) must continue throughout the disciple building process if we are going to help people grow. Accountability is important, but it must be wise accountability, meeting people where they are and encouraging them to take the next step. This is what Paul had in mind when he said, "We proclaim Him, admonishing and teaching everyone with all wisdom, so that we may present everyone perfect [mature] in Christ." (Colossians 1:28)

Jesus once again is our example. He wasn't afraid to get tough when the situation called for toughness (e.g. He turned over the tables of the money-changers). But He was also patient and forgiving when the occasion called for it (e.g. The woman caught in adultery). Before leaving, He promised to send "another like Himself" referring to the Holy Spirit. The Spirit is also called The Helper (Gk. "paracletos" the One who comes alongside us to help). Get the picture? He was sent to put His arm around our waist and give us someone to lean on. But the Scriptures also exhort us to bear one another's burden. Disciple builders must become "alongsiders," people who walk with the Spirit and encourage others, providing feedback and appropriate accountability.

P: *Prayer* Causes Growth to Occur

Earlier we discussed Phase V, the period of Jesus' ministry when the disciples struggled with pride and self-sufficiency. At this time Jesus revealed to Peter that the devil was out to get him and then He went on to say, "But I have prayed for you." (Luke 22:32) Jesus was constantly doing that: praying. He prayed all night before He selected The Twelve. He prayed after feeding the 5000, where Scripture tells us, "they had not gained any insight from the incident of the loaves, but their heart was hardened." (Mark 6:52, NASB) The Twelve were in the storm at sea, but Jesus was on the land, praying. The account says, "Seeing them straining at the oars, for the wind was against them, at about the fourth watch of the night He came to them, walking on the sea." (Mark 6:48, NASB) He prayed, lifting His eyes to heaven before raising Lazarus from the dead, and on and on. There are many references of Jesus, the Master Disciple Builder, praying.

And He exhorted His disciples to pray and not lose heart. He understood that prayer was part of spiritual warfare, pointing out that whenever two or more of us agree about a matter, God would put His seal of authority on the matter, binding or loosing whatever we bind or loose. He reminded His disciples that before entering the strong man's house and plundering his goods, the strong man had to be bound. He prayed for insight, for protection, for provision, for sovereign intervention. He prayed early in the morning and throughout the day.

Paul reminds us that teaching doctrine isn't enough. After a passage in his letter to the Ephesian church that is filled with wonderful insight regarding God and His Kingdom, Paul says, "I pray also that the eyes of your heart may be enlightened…" (Ephesians 1:18) In my estimation, prayer is the disciple building initiative most challenging to implement. I think this is true partly because we hate admitting that anything is beyond our control. By definition, prayer is our willingness to acknowledge we need God to intervene, to do things that are impossible for us. But prayer is also difficult due to spiritual warfare. Satan hates it when we pray. He understands the power of intercession.

We should encourage our disciples to pray, and we should pray with them. As with every other disciple building initiative, what we pray for changes as a disciple grows. I am always amazed at the prayers of young Christians. They tend to ask for the craziest things. But even more amazing, is that God often answers many of these zany requests. This shouldn't surprise us. God is intent on showing young Christians that He loves them and they can trust Him. For this reason He often answers the prayers of a less mature Christian differently than He might answer the prayers of a more mature Christian. Having an understanding of how prayer changes through the phases of growth is important. (For more details see the Exhibits at the end of this book.)

S: *Structured* Growth Situations

Jesus spoke of the importance of structures to accomplish the goals of the Kingdom. His admonition to put wine in the proper container is as important today as it was in the first century. Whether Jesus was in a home, on the road or in the Temple, He was continuously instructing His small band of disciples. His goal was clear: to equip them for the leadership of the church, which included reproducing themselves through others. Jesus trained the first church leaders in a dynamic school that was centered around relationships, with truth being taught in the context of real life situations.

Unfortunately, most seminaries have abandoned this relational model of leadership development for the classroom approach. Please don't misunderstand; there are many advantages to a seminary education. But we must recognize that the classic seminary model is not configured to instruct in the context of "real life" situations. While valuable as a means to impart information and technical skills, the classroom is less helpful in training in the development of character and conduct: the primary goals of Christian development. Some seminaries are attempting to change their approach, but the classroom/lecture method still prevails.

The type of training structure favored in academia has become the prototype for the church. Most of the small groups in the modern church meet as Sunday school classes. There is little opportunity for relational interaction in this type of structure. Though there is a movement toward home fellowship groups, the lecture format is often still the dominant style. The result is that people are instructed, but they are not held relationally accountable to put the truth they learn into practice. It is time to adopt a more comprehensive approach that integrates several types of structures to better accomplish the goal of applying truth, not merely understanding truth.

In the R-CAPS Grid the "S" refers to the specific "situations" that facilitate spiritual growth. The term "situations" describes the environment that is created by a particular set of events or circumstances. There are two different kinds of situations for growth that the disciple builder must be aware of.

Some of the situations of the Christian life are divinely arranged by the sovereign initiative of God. These events/circumstances are not under the control of the leader/disciple builder. When this occurs, the role of a wise disciple builder is to understand and cooperate with what God has planned and help the disciple respond in faith.

But other types of situations can be planned or constructed by the disciple builder. These constructed situations are also designed to create a faith-building experience for the disciple. At WDA, we refer to these constructed situations as "structures." Thus, when the disciple builder plans a specific event and challenges the disciple to be a part, he has created a "structure" for disciple building.

When used this way, the term "structures" includes all of the activities used by disciple builders to plan and organize a disciple building approach. All of the meetings, programs, activities, and scheduled events that make up the calendar of the disciple are included. These structured events may be as simple as an appointment over coffee with a friend, or as complex as a community-wide program or event lasting several days or weeks. But they are all intentional, planned and considered by leaders who desire to create opportunities for growth and development. It is the responsibility of the leadership to construct these structures as part of a complete disciple building regimen.

There are six distinct types of structures that form the framework for spiritual life and development. Five of these structures [A-E] should be incorporated into the scheduled activities of a local community of Christians. The sixth [F] should be incorporated into the ongoing spiritual disciplines of an individual disciple.

A. Small Groups

B. Life Coaching Relationships

C. Public Gatherings

D. Ministry Involvement / Activities

E. The Training School

F. Personal Growth Activities (or Spiritual Disciplines)

All of these together play an important role in our spiritual development though each is unique. The best arrangement for

Christian growth is when all of these structures work in concert with one another. (For a better understanding of how to achieve this, see *Disciple Building: Life Coaching*, WDA.)

It is important to note that whether a "situation" is structured or not, it is nonetheless key in the development of the disciple. Both types of situations, those structured by disciple builders and those initiated by God, create opportunities for growth. This may have been part of what Paul had in mind when he asserted in II Corinthians that he had planted, and Apollos had watered, but it was God who had caused the growth.

Addendum C
Emotional Healing Goals of Five Phases

Other WDA publications discuss this topic more thoroughly, but listed below are some of the restorative goals associated with the Five Phases. (For a more complete discussion of this dynamic and for help in addressing the emotional issues of disciple building visit our website www.disciplebuilding.org.)

Phase I: Establishing Faith

1. Understand and receive forgiveness

2. Begin a relationship with God

Phase II: Laying Foundations

1. Identify and correct distorted views of God

2. Develop self-awareness

3. Feel a part of a group

4. Understand a biblical view of man

5. Develop personal responsibility

6. Understand addictive behavior

7. Identify and learn to deal with emotions appropriately

8. Understand grieving and forgiveness

9. Identify personal needs and appropriate ways to meet them

10. Understand how the past affects the present

11. Learn to trust God and safe people

Phase III: Equipping For Ministry

1. Understand and apply the power of personal choice

2. Develop a healthy perspective on limits

3. Identify and overcome personal fears related to relationships and ministry

4. Develop healthy relationships and relationship skills

5. Learn to initiate in healthy ways toward others

6. Learn to take responsibility for personal problems and not the problems of others

7. Learn to address conflict appropriately

8. Develop comfort with and ability to be oneself

9. Feel accepted by God and not condemned

10. Become more aware of strengths and weaknesses

11. Balance time for self and others

12. Develop ability to not compromise the truth

13. Feel connected to others

Phase IV: Developing New Leaders

1. Learn healthy team and family dynamics

2. Develop negotiation and problem solving skills

3. Develop flexibility (not too rigid or out of control)

4. Develop perspective that to struggle and fail is human and not unique

5. Become a contributing member of a leadership team

6. Accept the idea that people and institutions are both good and bad

7. Learn to subordinate self to a group

8. Grow in ability to be a servant leader

9. Develop abilities to overcome relational problems

10. Beginning to identify one's spiritual gifts and passion

11. Develop realism (not overly critical or obsessive)

12. Understand the complexity of human problems and solutions

13. Understand that truth lies in tension with other truth

14. Understand that suffering is normal and is designed to produce good

Phase V: Developing Mature Leaders

1. Develop skills to lead a team

2. Develop personal ministry based on personal passion

3. Learn to appreciate the differences between people and the contribution that each makes

4. Develop a vision of how a team ministry can change the world

5. Learn that effective teams come from everyone doing their part

6. Learn that effective teams accomplish more than the sum of their parts

7. Learn to allow eternal matters and world vision to impact priorities and decisions

8. Learn to determine God's will as a team

9. Develop belief that God can sovereignly supply all the team needs to accomplish His will

CHILDHOOD EXPERIENCES AFFECT SPIRITUAL GROWTH IN ADULTS

Our personal development (process of maturity) begins in childhood. There are a number of abilities and skills in the area of emotional and relational development we need to learn in childhood. The family is the primary training environment for this to happen. Ideally, the culture will also encourage these qualities.

Because of the breakdown of the family and the corresponding deterioration of culture, often children are not able to get what they need today. Even in healthier families (those that stay together and are more nurturing) parents are often not able to give their children what they need because they never got what they needed when they were children. (It is difficult to transfer to others what you don't have or communicate concepts you are unaware of. Ironically, many parents become so focused on their own needs and survival that they are oblivious to their children's needs.)

THE FOUR DEVELOPMENTAL TASKS OF CHILDHOOD

Disciple builders need to be aware of four skills critical for emotional and relational balance, that should be developed during childhood. If these skills (often referred to by psychologists as "developmental tasks") are not adequately developed, they can become a leading cause of spiritual problems later in life. Even if these tasks were completed adequately during childhood, they still need to be reinforced and applied in adult life. A healthy Christian disciple building environment is invaluable for reinforcing these skills and for helping adults complete any unfinished skills. There is strong evidence to suggest that the progressive disciple building ministry of Christ was intentionally designed to enhance and supplement the emotional development of childhood. Each of the Phases (beginning with Phase II) can be linked with one of the developmental tasks.

1. Bonding—Bonding is the process by which children (from birth to nine months) learn to connect with the people who care for them. Through thousands of interactions with parents, the child develops a sense of connection with them. If all progresses well, the child will see himself as an extension of his parents and not as an independent person. This is healthy at this stage. Throughout this period, as parents emotionally bond with their child, a number of messages will normally and naturally be internalized by the child, including:

1. I am loved.

2. My feelings and needs are OK.

3. I can trust others to meet my needs.

Once these messages are internalized, the child can start to move away from their parents (separate) and still believe these messages without the need for them to be constantly reinforced. If bonding does not occur, or if these messages become distorted or replaced, the child will usually have problems connecting with others as an adult. There may be difficulty connecting because he cannot accept love, does not trust others, or is out of touch with his feelings and needs and thus denies his need for others.

This task corresponds to Phase II of spiritual growth, Laying Foundations. In this early phase Jesus gathered a small group of followers, and He spent the next six to nine months building a relationship with them. Establishing fellowship with them seemed to be His primary emphasis, more important at this time than involving them in ministry. He revealed who He was to them, spent ample time with them and offered them grace, acceptance, and hope.

Essentially, Jesus and His new disciples became a new (surrogate) family and did what all new families need to do: they bonded with one another. This new, spiritual family provided an ideal environment for His disciples to complete the task of bonding if they had not previously done so. It also served to help the new Christians address any wounds they may have sustained from inadequate bonding as children.

2. Separating—Separating is the beginning of the process in which children form their own individual identity. Psychologists tell us that this happens between the ages of nine months and six years. During this period children begin to pull away from their parents and experiment with individuality. As they become more mobile, they can do more things. Children are normally able to pull away and still feel connected and secure if they have internalized the bonding messages.

If a person fails to form a separate and strong sense of identity, she may face some of the following problems:

1. A general lack of self-understanding and direction in life (identity confusion).

2. Relational problems such as being too dependent on others, being too isolated from others, feeling overly responsible for others, or becoming a caretaker of others.

3. Significant boundary problems; allowing others to take advantage of her or overpower her. Or, she may take advantage of or overpower others.

This task corresponds to Phase III of Christian growth, Equipping For Ministry. At the beginning of Phase III Jesus challenged His men to follow Him and become fishers of men (Matthew 4:19). He then took them on a series of evangelistic tours where they ministered alongside Him. They were no longer merely spectators, watching Him minister (cf. Phase II). At this phase, they were involved in ministering to others also. They were beginning to develop their own spiritual identity. In the later phases of growth Jesus continued to expand their ministry experiences allowing them to further develop their ministry abilities. This helped them define and clarify their spiritual identity, and reminded them of how God had uniquely created them to fit into His Kingdom.

Any of Jesus' disciples who had not yet been able to fully develop their separate identities would have the opportunity to complete this task while learning to minister to others. This process began in this phase and continued through the remaining phases of growth.

3. Sorting Out Good and Bad—People who do not complete this task tend to see things as either all good or all bad. For them, everything is black or white. There are no shades of gray. The problem is they cannot tolerate bad in themselves or in others. But neither we, others, nor the world around us, are all good or all bad. Everything contains a mixture of both good and bad. The Fall marred creation and the image of God in people, but it did not obliterate this image.

If we are unable to make a balanced distinction between good and bad, it is a sign that we have not completed this skill. Consequently, we will tend to have one or more of the following problems:

1. **Deny the Good**—This person has the tendency to blame himself for everything bad that happens. He actually sees himself as totally bad. He denies his worth and/or his ability to contribute anything good. He may elevate others to a position of being better than he is, or he may be critical of others, judging them as totally bad also.

2. **Deny the Bad**—This person cannot tolerate the notion that he is ever wrong, because this is the equivalent of admitting he is bad, and therefore worthless. He must doggedly deny the existence of bad in himself, blaming others for anything bad that happens while justifying himself. This person has great difficulty acknowledging his own faults.

3. **All Good to All Bad**—This person tends to see people and situations as "all good" at first, but later, after experiencing

problems, he sees the same people and situations as "all bad." The truth is that people and situations are both good and bad at first, and good and bad later. As a result of this distortion, this person often initially views a new relationship, church, or job as perfect, but as intolerable later, as reality sets in. He keeps changing relationships, churches, and jobs looking for the "perfect" situation.

This task corresponds to Phase IV, Developing New Leaders. In this phase of growth Jesus lays out for His immediate disciples, who have just been appointed as leaders in His ministry and designated to be apostles, what He expects of them in terms of heart righteousness in the Sermon on the Mount. They must begin at this point in their growth to wrestle with their inability to fully keep the law as Jesus defines it in the Sermon on the Mount. Jesus raises the bar so high that no one can reach the moral standards He has set.

He also began to expose the legalistic and hypocritical practices and attitudes of the Pharisees and Scribes. They claimed to keep the law but were miserable failures. It was important for the apostles to accept the fact that no one could completely keep the law, but everyone still needed to try. They needed to accept that they could sin less, but never be sinless.

In addition, there was a dramatic rise in the persecution Jesus and His followers were experiencing. All of this continued to cause them to re-evaluate their expectations of the Christian life. They needed to come to grips with the fact that they were good and bad and that no matter how much progress they made against sin, they would still remain both good and bad until the final Resurrection. They needed to accept the fact that the fallen world was never going to accept Jesus and be completely changed. They were in a spiritual battle that was not going to go away. They could make an impact, but Satan would remain the ruler of this world until the return of Christ.

If any of Jesus' disciples had not completed this developmental task, this phase of growth gave them an opportunity to work further on this issue. All the issues surrounding this matter are brought to the surface again and can be dealt with more completely.

4. Gaining Independence—This last developmental task occurs during adolescence. This is when a child moves from a "dependent" relationship with her parents and other adults (a situation where she has limited authority, freedom and choice), to more of an "equal" relationship with these people. This is a process that happens slowly. It is supposed to be completed as the child leaves home, moves out on her own, and takes total responsibility for her own life. Some adults never complete this task. They continue to be dependent on their parents and other adults. As a result they continue to feel less mature than other adults.

If this task is not completed, several of the following characteristics are usually present.

1. An inordinate need for approval

2. A fear of disapproval

3. A crippling fear of failure

4. A need for permission to be given, before initiating action

5. A feeling of inferiority

6. A loss of power or control (which is often given away to others)

7. An over-dependence on others

8. An idealization of people in authority

This task corresponds to Phase V, Developing Mature Leaders. During this period of time Jesus appointed a second group of leaders, The Seventy (Luke 10). The Twelve are now helping Him lead this new group of leaders and continue to reach out to new groups of people. Jesus, because He is doing a lot more work with The Seventy, begins to withdraw from The Twelve while giving them more authority. The result is that The Twelve developed more independence from Jesus and gained more authority in the ministry. At the end of this period, Jesus left them and went back to Heaven, leaving them in charge.

This is exactly what is needed for those who feel inferior to others. They need to be able to understand their authority and begin to exercise it. They need to establish their independence and take authority over their lives. They need to establish an equal role with those who are in authoritative positions with them. They need to come out from under people's authority and establish their own. Only as we complete this task are we able to show proper respect for and submission to the authorities God places over us.

Jesus' ministry allowed any of His disciples who had not yet completed this task of becoming an adult to do so. It was an opportunity to establish their independence and equal authority with other adults.

WE NEED BETTER PARENTING SKILLS

It would be helpful if more churches trained parents in strategies that could help them pass on healthy styles of relating to their children. Another benefit of the disciple building process at work in the church occurs as parents begin to grow, addressing their emotional and relational needs. The resulting maturity filters down through the family and provides a better atmosphere for dealing with the issues facing the children.

Fortunately, there are a number of things we can do to make families healthier. These include developing strategies for appropriately empowering our children, teaching children how to deal with negative emotions, teaching children how to grieve and how to have a balanced approach to forgiveness, teaching children how to stand up for themselves in healthy ways. We can create healthy support systems for our children, teaching healthy views of self, the world, and God.

Healing from emotional and relational damage will take time, but people who begin to address these issues find that their life (including their walk with God) improves significantly. Restorative growth is very healing and empowering. It is life transforming. Unfortunately, some people are so damaged they will have trouble growing spiritually even if we provide the support they need. They may have to focus almost exclusively on emotional restoration at first. Eventually, the spiritual dimension will also develop, but only if proper care is provided. Some disciples may require the help of a professional counselor. Fortunately, most people will be restored from much of the damage of the past if we can incorporate emotional and relational healing into a biblical disciple building process.

Addendum D
Disciple Building and Classic Revivalism

We need a structured disciple building approach that promotes progressive, sustained spiritual growth / renewal while operating in concert with the special work of the Spirit often associated with classic revivalism. For this to occur, balance and wisdom are needed. The process of spiritual development is, in some ways, mysterious and beyond our ability to comprehend (John 3:8). But the priority of facilitating growth is communicated straightforwardly in Scripture and is clearly within our scope of responsibility (Jude 1:20; Colossians 1:28-29).

Growth and renewal seem to occur from two directions. There is the ongoing renewal that occurs as Christians are built up through the "normal" work of the Spirit as He operates in and through the body of Christ, the church. At other times there are "special," spontaneous outpourings of God's Spirit that supersede the normal workings. It is our contention that spiritual leaders need to pray for both, and create structures (or wineskins) that facilitate both.

Jesus pointed out the relationship between wineskins and new wine, speaking metaphorically of the need for a new structure to accommodate a new ministry of the Holy Spirit. At one level He was pointing to the emergence of the church, a brand new structure similar to, but distinct from, Judaism. At another level He was emphasizing the important relationship between right structures and spiritual renewal. He warned that dispensations of God's grace can become traditions that tend to harden over time. Fresh outpourings of grace require pliable (new) structural models. The forms or structures of the church are an important part of the ministry of renewal that takes place within the church.

The church at the beginning of the New Millennium is looking and hoping for renewal. For many this means an outpouring of grace that enables the people of God to awaken from complacency and defeat and enter a new phase in their relationship with God characterized by renewed zeal and holiness. This hope is not unfounded. The history of the church in recent centuries has been marked by such spiritual awakenings. These periods of renewal are definitive, sweeping, and marked by discernible evidence of increased commitment. Unfortunately, they are also characterized as being short-lived, lacking in their ability to sustain zeal and ensure spiritual maturity. This raises the question: "Is there any way to promote ongoing spiritual renewal among God's people?"

The answer is a resounding YES! God has given us a pattern and strategy for spiritual development and renewal. Though not entirely predictable, this pattern is nonetheless definitive and able to be structured. Without sacrificing His sovereignty, God has provided wineskins that balance divine initiatives with human stewardship, supporting a process of ongoing growth to maturity.

At first glance, historical awakenings seem entirely spontaneous or totally God-initiated. But a closer look reveals that often there were specific acts of obedience undertaken by the people of God prior to the period of renewal. Acts of consecration, intense prayer, fasting, and preaching-teaching often preceded the moment when (special) renewal/revival began to occur. If this is true, might there be corresponding acts of obedience to sustain ongoing (normal) renewal? Of course we must avoid trying to reduce God or His acts to a formula. He is sovereign and unpredictable, reserving the right to act completely separate from His Creation. But this does not preclude His consigning to His church the responsibility to carry out His divine plan by responding in obedience to His directives.

While there may not be a "formula" for revival, there do appear to be catalysts. Accounts of revivals, both contemporary and classical, have been documented and explored by Christian authors in an attempt to discover specific pre-conditions that accompanied awakenings. Dr. Richard Lovelace spent much of his academic career studying the history and theology of religious awakenings. In his book *Dynamics of Spiritual Life*, Lovelace lists specific stewardships that affect the spiritual life of God's people and characterize periods of renewal and impact for the church.

Dr. Lovelace reminds us that a primary focus within the historical tradition was *ecclesia reformata semper reformanda* (A reformed church, always reforming). According to Lovelace, the Puritans and Pietists, building on the traditions of Augustine, affirmed that "the pre-condition of perpetual reformation is the spiritual revitalization of the church." In other words, a church that has in place systems or structures for ongoing spiritual development will become the ideal climate for spiritual health and renewal. A church that is fully awake, doesn't need to be awakened.

Many of the elements for ongoing renewal mentioned in *Dynamics* are coincidentally the fundamentals of Christian discipleship. There is a direct link between discipleship and ongoing revival. In fact, revival is going on at one level constantly within the church. As individual Christians become more mature, the church corporate becomes more mature and reflects the image of Christ in a dark and dying world.

This is not to say that spontaneous, corporate revivals are not important. Certainly history and personal experience attest to the value of God's special visitations and spiritual outpourings. The tendency toward spiritual entropy will exist as long as we live in our fallen state, so the need for periodic renewal certainly remains. But revivalist models should not replace models of ongoing renewal. Church leaders must adopt strategies that allow both approaches to work in concert. Ironically, if we neglect ongoing renewal (disciple building) models, a subsequent need arises for spontaneous revivals to address the resultant spiritual coldness and latent immaturity.

The church is most healthy when God's appointed leaders adopt a strategy that includes both ongoing renewal through strategic disciple building and the appeal for special outpourings to augment and enhance the salt and light effect of "normal" life in the body of Christ. We must fast and pray that God will send these special outpourings. But we must also work for personal revival and ongoing restoration through the discipline of making disciples.

Exhibit 1
What Jesus Did, What We Can Do

Exhibit 1

Phase I: Establishing Faith

Primary Goal: To reach out to non-Christians and proclaim the Gospel in an effort to establish faith in Christ alone for salvation, and conduct basic follow-up with new Christians.

What Jesus Did		What We Can Do
Jesus and John the Baptist: •Went to the lost sheep of Israel and showed concern and care for their spiritual condition by delivering a tough message, laced with love •Gathered people who needed to hear the message and those who had responded to the message *Isaiah 40:3 cf. 42:3/Matthew 9:12 "I have come to call sinners."*	**Relationships**	•Build relationships with non-Christians in an attempt to "connect"
•Taught God's love, holiness, the atonement of the Lamb of God, the future judgment, the role of the Holy Spirit, evangelistic apologetics, and the divine nature of Christ *John 1:29-34 "Behold the Lamb of God who takes away the sin of the world."*	**Content**	•Share with non-Christians the Good News and answer their questions about the Christian faith •Follow up with those who respond
•Called people to repent, turn away from contemporary idols and put their trust in God's deliverer (Messiah) •Exhorted the people to become followers (disciples) of this Promised One *Matthew 3:1-2 "Repent, for the Kingdom of Heaven is near."*	**Accountability**	•Challenge people to repent, accept Christ and publicly declare their faith in Him

What Jesus Did		What We Can Do
•Asked God to call men to become Christ's disciples •Asked that the strong man would be bound and the power of the enemy broken so the Word might be proclaimed *Matthew 16:19 "Whatever you bind on earth will be bound in heaven."*	**Prayer**	•Pray for opportunities to share Christ with non-Christians •Pray and prepare for the spiritual attacks •Pray that people will become aware of their own emotional needs
•Had various evangelistic encounters and situations where relationships could be established •Had large groups, small groups (in homes and at public gatherings) and individual contacts *Matthew 9:10 "While Jesus was having dinner at Matthew's house, many tax collectors and sinners came and ate with Him and His disciples."*	**Situations**	•Conduct evangelistic outreaches in communities •Hold evangelistic socials in our homes and churches •Provide opportunities for new disciples to publicly confess their faith in Christ

Scriptures from The Harmony of the Gospels:
Matthew 3:1 - 4:11; Mark 1:1-13; Luke 2:1-2, 3:3-18,21-23, 4:1-13; John 1:19-28

Exhibit 1

Phase II: Laying Foundations

Primary Goal: To gather young Christians into a small group to help them understand the foundational truths of the Christian life and involve them in the larger Christian community.

What Jesus Did   ## What We Can Do

Relationships

•Challenged a group of disciples to be with Him •Spent time with them individually and as a group •Revealed His identity as Messiah

John 1:39 "Rabbi, where are you staying?" "Come and you will see!"

•Gather an "open" group of young Christians who desire to grow •Begin spending time getting to know each of them •Create an honest, safe, grace-oriented, sharing environment that facilitates trust & emotional safety

Content

•Revealed Himself to them as the Messiah through His teaching and miracles •Taught that the Kingdom of God under Messianic rule had appeared and that God had provided an opportunity for them to participate

John 2:11 "He thus revealed His glory, and His disciples put their faith in Him."

•Teach new disciples the "foundational truths" of the Christian life: The person and work of Christ, the ministry of the Holy Spirit, the sovereign plan of God, and how to grow spiritually

Accountability

•Challenged them to put their faith fully in Him as their Teacher and Guide •Challenged some to become His followers

John 1:43 "Finding Phillip He said to him, 'Follow me.'"

•Challenge them to be committed to learning how to grow by having a Quiet Time and being around other Christians •Invite them to participate in a small group •Encourage them to share emotions & needs •Identify emotional trauma & faulty belief systems •Encourage them to look to God to meet their needs in answer to their specific prayers

What Jesus Did		What We Can Do
• Asked God the Father to call men to follow Him and reveal that He was the Christ •Prayed that power would be made available to accomplish attesting miracles *John 1:47ff. (to Nathaniel) "I saw you when you were under the fig tree...you shall see... angels ascending and descending on the Son of Man."*	**Prayer**	•Ask God to reveal Himself to these new disciples in powerful and intimate ways, answering their prayers and helping them gain insights into His nature and power
•Performed miracles attesting to His divine nature and authority •Set up various teaching situations both publicly and privately •Established His Messianic authority over Israel by cleansing the Temple •Formed a group of followers and took them with Him as He taught and performed miracles *John 3:2 (Nicodemus) "Rabbi, no one could perform the miraculous signs you are doing if God were not with him!"*	**Situations**	•Provide opportunities for new followers to become involved in the Christian community by delegating logistical tasks •Provide social functions to establish relationships with more mature Christians •Assign an accountability partner •Be prepared for the Lord to precipitate specific needs that He will provide for

Scriptures from The Harmony of the Gospels:
Matthew 4:12-17; Mark 1:14-15; Luke 3:19-20, 4:14-31; John 1:29 - 4:54

Exhibit 1

Phase III: Equipping for Ministry

Primary Goal: To equip the disciples for ministry in the Kingdom and learn more about the nature of the Kingdom and the principles which govern their role as citizens who are sons and daughters.

What Jesus Did		What We Can Do
•Challenged a few of His disciples to participate in His mission of winning the souls of people •Allowed them to follow Him into spiritual battles and observe His power and authority •Trained them as apprentices working alongside a Master *Mark 1:16ff. "He saw Simon and his brother Andrew casting a net into the sea...and said to them, 'Come, follow Me, and I will send you out to fish for people.'"*	**Relationships**	•Encourage our disciples to be with us as we model a ministry lifestyle •Model healthy relationships •Set & respect boundaries •Be willing to confront others in a caring way •Maintain priorities, and model other aspects of healthy relationships
•Stressed the importance of telling others about His mission and love for sinners •Trained them in basic ministry skills •Gave them insights into the nature of His Kingdom: He was Conqueror over the kingdom of darkness; had authority to forgive sin, heal sickness, and dispel demons *Luke 5:23ff. "Which is easier to say, 'Your sins are forgiven....'?"*	**Content**	•Offer training in evangelism skills •Teach about the sovereign authority of Christ over the spiritual realm and the traditions of men •Review the truths of the Gospel with the purpose of helping others understand •Teach and model healthy relationships •Teach about positional truth
•Called His disciples to be fishers of men •Challenged them to leave their worldly pursuits (at least temporarily) and follow Him on mission *Matthew 4:20 "At once they left their nets and followed Him."*	**Accountability**	•Challenge people to go with us as we reach out to the lost in our community •Challenge them to get training in how to win others to Christ •Encourage them to participate in various ministry situations •Construct projects that address emotional/spiritual strongholds

What Jesus Did | What We Can Do

What Jesus Did		What We Can Do
•Prayed for healing power and deliverance for those trapped in sin and satanic strongholds •Asked for their eyes to be opened to see and understand the spiritual battles raging around them •Prayed for another generation of disciples to repent and follow Him *II Kings 6 (Elisha's servant) cf. Matthew 16:13-19*	**Prayer**	•Ask God to open doors for our disciples to share their faith •Pray God would give them a vision and burden for the lost •Ask God to free them from emotional and relational bondage
•Took His disciples on a short-term mission project to upper Galilee •Challenged the status quo of religious traditions and human philosophies •Healed the sick and cast out demons *Matthew 4:23 "Jesus went throughout Galilee, teaching in their Synagogues, preaching the Good News of the Kingdom, and healing every disease and sickness."* *John 3:2 (Nicodemus) "Rabbi…no one could perform the miraculous signs you are doing if God were not with him!"*	**Situations**	•Take our disciples with us as we minister •Make time to debrief after our ministry times together •Offer opportunities to focus on ministry events, thus showing a willingness to change traditions for the sake of extending the Kingdom (retreats, concerts of prayer, evangelism training, mission projects, restorative opportunities, etc)

Scriptures from The Harmony of the Gospels:
Matthew 4:13-25, 8:2-4,14-17, 9:1-17, 12:1-21; Mark 1:16 - 3:12; Luke 4:31 - 6:11; John 5:1-47

Exhibit 1

Phase IV: Developing New Leaders

Primary Goal: To appoint a group of leaders and train them to apply kingdom principles as they assist in the ministry and help others grow.

What Jesus Did		What We Can Do
•Appointed the Twelve to be with Him as leaders in His ministry •Allowed them to assume important ministry roles and gave them authority •Sent them out in pairs to preach and minister in His Name •Spent extra time instructing them as a group and individually *Luke 6:13 "He called His disciples to Him and chose twelve of them."*	**Relationships**	•Appoint leaders •Train leaders as they assume roles of responsibility in the overall ministry and over individuals •Be prepared to provide encouraging perspective when God challenges their status quo
•Taught the principles of Kingdom life as being distinct from religious traditions •Explained that true religion was from the heart and not merely external acts •Taught the eternal nature of God's plan and purpose and the wisdom of placing priority on eternal over temporal matters •Taught principles of spiritual authority and warfare *Matthew 5-7 (Sermon on the Mount)*	**Content**	•Teach basic leadership skills •Explain that true discipleship will produce Christlikeness and that biblical ministry involves growth in character, not just success in ministry programs •Teach about spiritual warfare, problem solving, team dynamics and how to resolve conflict
•Challenged their human propensity to put their trust in themselves and the temporal systems of men •Tested them by disrupting their life and ministry •Jeopardized the success of His public ministry to emphasize the importance of internal obedience, faith, and eternal priorities *John 6:5 "Where shall we buy bread for these people to eat?"*	**Accountability**	•Allow our disciples to fail •Challenge them to assume responsibility in ministry tasks that appear bigger than their abilities •Help them rearrange their priorities around their new responsibilities

What Jesus Did

What We Can Do

Prayer

• Prayed that God would give wisdom in selecting the disciples who were ready for leadership • Asked that they might see the greatness of God and their own insufficiency and that God would provide supernaturally

Luke 6:12 "Jesus went out to a mountainside to pray, and spent the night praying to God. When morning came...."

• Pray for wisdom in the leadership selection process • Ask that they might see the greatness of God and their own insufficiency • Ask God to provide for them supernaturally

Situations

• Gave them real responsibilities in His ministry • Set up ministry situations that required supernatural provision and demanded faith • Created a new structure in His ministry: the Leadership Team which allowed Him opportunities to apply truth at a deeper level by instructing these leaders separately from the main body of disciples and/or the interested others • Required them to spend more time with Him and the work, thus causing them to reevaluate their priorities

John 6 "Do not work for the food which perishes, but...endures."

• Help them develop the gifts God has given them by positioning them in roles that suit them • Send them into situations that will be sure to invite spiritual warfare • Give them responsibilities to disciple and mentor young Christians • Include them in the Leadership Team

©WDA 1997-2019

Scriptures from The Harmony of the Gospels:
Matthew 5:1 - 17:23; Mark 3:13 - 9:32; Luke 6:12 - 9:45; John 6:1 - 7:1

103

Exhibit 1

Phase V: Developing Mature Leaders

Primary Goal: To develop a group of mature disciples who have a vision for reaching the nations through God's enabling power, and to have an ability to make other disciples according to the pattern Jesus used.

What Jesus Did		What We Can Do
•Reduced their dependence on him while continuing to have an intimate relationship with them by giving them more independence and slowly weaning them from Himself •Challenged them to be committed to one another •Washed their feet •Laid down His life on the Cross *John 15:15-17 "I have called you friends, for everything that I learned from My Father I have made known to you. ...Love each other."*	**Relationships**	•Focus our training and attention on our disciples' full development •Commission them as peers in ministry •Continue to serve and love them as friends
•Taught the importance of reaching all the nations, the all-sufficiency of the Spirit, the inadequacy of human strength, the importance of unity in the Body, how the church should function and how to demonstrate agape love in the midst of relational struggles *John 17:23 "May they be brought to complete unity to let the world know that you sent me...."*	**Content**	•Teach the importance of unity, reaching the nations, suffering love, and (advanced) leadership skills •Teach the dynamics of family life and church life •Remind them that though they have been trained, discipleship is never fully completed until we stand before Christ
•Challenged them to love one another •Commanded them to feed and care for His sheep •Challenged them to go into the entire world and make disciples *John 15:17 "This is my command: Love each other."*	**Accountability**	•Challenge them to consider what worldwide mission involvement would look like for them •Exhort them to set aside petty differences and strive to put each other first •Suggest they become less dependent on us as mentors and form new ministry relationships

What Jesus Did		What We Can Do
•Prayed they would be able to overcome the enemy and their fleshly self-sufficiency •Asked that they would experience the fullness and enabling of the Holy Spirit *Luke 22:31 "Simon, Simon, Satan has asked to sift you like wheat. But I have prayed for you."*	**Prayer**	•Pray God would allow them to humbly rest in the power of Christ's Spirit in them •Ask for unity and love to prevail as the enemy puts stress on relationships •Ask God to give them a vision and burden for the entire world
•Gave them increased responsibility in leading the ministry •Moved His ministry beyond the borders of Palestine •Commanded them to go into the entire world to make disciples and then teach these disciples to put into practice the same things they had been taught *Matthew 28:18-20 "Go and make disciples of all nations...."*	**Situations**	•Include them as part of a leadership team that directs the larger ministry •Take the Great Commission seriously by setting up discipleship training and world missions opportunities •Watch for the Lord to put our disciples, and us, in situations where they/we are incapable of pulling ministry off in our own strength

Scriptures from The Harmony of the Gospels:
Matthew 17:24 - 28:20; Mark 9:33 - 16:20; Luke 9:46 - 24:53; John 7:2 - 21:25; Acts 1:1 - 2:4

Exhibit 2
R-CAPS Grid
Strategy for the Disciple Builder

Exhibit 2

R-CAPS Grid Strategy for the Disciple Builder

Phases of Christian Growth:	Phase *I* Establishing Faith		Phase *II* Laying Foundations
	Part A Cultivating Interest	**Part B** Providing Follow-up	

	New Christian ▶		Young Christian ▶
R *Relationships*	Showing Concern 1	Initiating 6	Nurturing 11
C *Content*	Gospel 2	Follow-up 7	Foundational Truths 12
A *Accountability*	Seeks God, Repents and Believes 3	Begins to Grow 8	Cultivates Relationships with God and Christians 13
P *Prayer*	Salvation 4	Assurance 9	Understanding and Growth 14
S *Situations*	Opportunity to respond to Gospel 5	Opportunity to Break with Old Life 10	Involvement in Body of Christ 15

Phase *III*
Equipping for Ministry

Phase *IV*
Developing New Leaders

Phase *V*
Developing Mature Leaders

| | **Part A**
Appointing
New Leaders | **Part B**
Focusing on
Eternal
Things | **Part A**
Delegating
New Respon-
sibilities | **Part B**
Casting a
World Vision |

Ministry Trainee ▶ **New Leader** ▶ **Mature Leader**

Mentoring 16	Training 21	Encouraging 26	Delegating 31	Commis- sioning 36
Law and Grace 17	Leadership Principles: Character, Authority 22	Eternal Perspective 27	Team Ministry 32	Resurrection Power in Daily Life 37
Becomes Ministry-Minded 18	Assumes Leadership Responsibili- ties 23	Adjusts Expectations 28	Fosters Unity 33	Shows Sacri- ficial Love to Reach the World 38
Courage/Provision 19	Perspective/ Wisdom 24	Endurance 29	Unity in Diversity 34	Sacrificial Love 39
Opportunity to Serve and Witness 20	Appoint- ment to Leadership Role 25	Acceptance of Difficult Assignments 30	Ability to Work with Other Leaders 35	Acceptance of Worldwide Challenge 40

Exhibit 3
R-CAPS Legend
Strategy for the Disciple Builder

Phase I: Establishing Faith

PART A—CULTIVATING INTEREST

Showing Concern (R) Disciple Builder:

1a   Goes into non-Christian's world: relates in casual, social situations; develops friendships with those who are open; shows compassion; meets felt needs.

1b   Invites those who are curious to get together in groups.

1c   Is transparent about his beliefs in the normal course of conversation. Doesn't hide who he is, but also doesn't press his views.

Disciple Builder: The goal here is to show non-Christians the love of Christ. You should enter into their world and show love, compassion and genuine interest. Show them in practical ways that the love of Jesus is relevant and sufficient to meet their needs. Also, be available to answer questions.

Gospel (C) Disciple Builder:

2a   Addresses felt needs from a biblical perspective: relationships, self-esteem, career, etc. as a way of showing God's love and holiness.

2b   Answers questions and objections (apologetics).

2c   Presents plan of salvation: e.g., God's justice, wrath, judgment, love, mercy, grace and forgiveness; Christ's substitution; and our need for genuine repentance and faith.

Exhibit 3

Disciple Builder: It's important to focus on meeting a person's felt needs—areas he wants help in (marriage, parenting, finances, etc.). Address these from a biblical perspective as interest and the relationship allow. That is, if the person is somewhat hostile to spiritual issues, you might not directly refer to what the Bible says about a particular issue. Be sensitive.

When a person is interested in spiritual things, the leader can introduce him to more biblical information. However, it is important that the leader be sure that this biblical information is presented in understandable, relevant terms (not Christian jargon that may be meaningless or overwhelming). The person needs to know the basics of God's character and how to become a Christian. You as the leader need to discern what is holding the person back and plan appropriately. (For example, if it is a heart/willingness issue, you may need to pray and continue being a friend. If there is a specific issue hindering the person, you may need to help resolve that issue.)

Seeks God, Repents and Believes (A) Non-Christian:

3a   Shows interest in knowing more about God (e.g., responds to an invitation to a Christian event).

3b   Begins to think about God and ask questions.

3c   Confesses, repents and puts faith in God (makes restitution, if necessary).

Disciple Builder: To become a Christian, the person must repent and make a decision to follow Christ. His life will begin to change, and you will begin to see fruit. Do not rush this transition. Genuine repentance is essential to growth.

Salvation (P) Disciple Builder prays:

4a   For open doors, boldness and words to speak.

4b   For God to break down strongholds and build interest in non-Christian.

4c   For repentance and faith in God (for non-Christian to see sin, believe in God's judgment, understand God's message of repentance, understand and respond to God's love and forgiveness, gain respect for God and His Word, and for God to expose idols in the person's life).

Disciple Builder: Much of the work will be done by the Holy Spirit in the person's heart. Prayer is essential.

Opportunity to Respond to Gospel (S) Disciple Builder:

5a   Puts non-Christian or new Christian in situations in which he can experience God's love and character through Christians. For example: invites non-Christian to evangelistic Bible study (or meets one-to-one to discuss a study); invites to socials, etc. with Christians.

5b   Looks for situations in which disciple builder can help meet the person's needs.

Disciple Builder: Usually you will be with non-Christians or new Christians in daily situations of life (at the gym, dinner after work, a coffee break, a camping trip, etc.), not special religious events. Be sensitive to the person's level of interest and do not push him. Also, ask the person to help you with something (a household repair or another area he has expertise in). This willingness to ask for help demonstrates a humility that is attractive and builds the relationship. As a person becomes interested in spiritual things, you can be more direct by inviting him to Bible studies, etc. Again, however, you need to be careful not to overwhelm him with information or pressure him to make a commitment.

PART B—PROVIDING FOLLOW-UP

Initiating (R) Disciple Builder:

6a   Intentionally initiates with the new Christian in order to begin the follow-up process.

Exhibit 3

6b   Continues to develop a casual friendship with new Christian.

Follow-Up (C) Disciple Builder:

7a   Shares basic follow-up information: assurance of salvation, baptism, fellowship with other Christians, importance of the Word, basics of prayer and Bible study.

7b   Teaches benefits of following Christ: fellowship in Christ, eternal security in Christ.

Disciple Builder: These are the truths that form the basis of the life and growth of a Christian. The author of Hebrews refers to the "elementary teachings" in Hebrews 6:1. Understanding and beginning to live these truths is essential since Christlikeness is the goal.

Begins to Grow (A) Christian:

8a   Begins to grow: associates with other Christians, grows in assurance in relationship with Christ, takes steps to learn more.

8b   Begins to practice repentance daily (life begins to change); demonstrates humility.

8c   Publicly identifies with Christ and His body (through baptism).

Disciple Builder: At this point, you will begin to see changes in the new Christian's life. It is difficult to list specific changes to look for because they vary based on the person's need and the sovereign choice of God. However, the changes will occur primarily in the areas of attitude toward God and others. Some "sin" areas (especially habits that are deeply ingrained) may remain because the new Christian is still quite young in his relationship with God. Be careful not to expect too much too soon or to impose legalistic standards. The person is ready to move on to Phase II: Laying Foundations when he understands and has begun to practice the follow-up truths.

Assurance (P) Disciple Builder prays:

9a   For protection as the gospel takes hold.

9b   For a teachable heart.

9c   For new Christian to be in situations in which he can see God at work in and for him.

9d   For new Christian to understand the assurance of his salvation, his eternal security, the fact that God loves him, the forgiveness of his sins, the fact that the Holy Spirit dwells in him, that the Bible is the Word of God.

Disciple Builder: Many ingredients go into the new Christian's growth in his new life in Christ: enjoying fellowship with other Christians, becoming acquainted with the Bible, understanding what God has done in his life, getting to know Jesus, dealing with sin areas in his life, etc. Prayer is essential as the new Christian and the disciple builder look to God as the source of growth.

Opportunity to Break with Old Life (S) Disciple Builder:

10a   Invites new Christian to attend a small group (or one-to-one appointments) for follow-up study.

10b   Looks for opportunities for the new Christian to fellowship with Christians.

10c   Gives new Christian the opportunity to confess his new faith in various situations.

Disciple Builder: It should not be expected that the new Christian's testimony be smooth or technically perfect at this point in his development. (At Phase III: Equipping For Ministry, time will be spent sharing how to prepare a testimony.) The purpose of giving the new Christian opportunities to talk about what God has done in his life (salvation) is to encourage him and solidify the commitment he has made.

Exhibit 3

Phase II: Laying Foundations

Nurturing (R) Disciple Builder:

11a Begins leading an open and safe group (i.e., people may come and go) in which relationships can develop (informal; not a long-term personal commitment).

11b Gives new disciple a chance to grow in love for and commitment to other Christians.

11c Continues to develop a trust relationship with disciple. Begins to model tasks (using the "steps of transfer" listed below) undertaken in the ministry (witnessing, sharing testimony). The relationship is casual, but disciple builder is available.

Disciple Builder: The term "steps of transfer" refers to the procedure used in training a disciple in a skill or activity. The steps of transfer are: Observation (O), Participation (P), Supervision (S), and Independence (I). Note that the abbreviation "OPSI" is used in this Legend. At the step of Observation, a disciple watches as the leader performs a task or activity. At the Participation step, she performs the task or activity with the leader. In the Supervision step, a disciple performs the task or activity alone, but with the supervision of the leader. At the last step of transfer, Independence, a disciple works on her own, independent of the disciple builder.

The commitment referred to in 11a and 11b is not an extensive, formal commitment, but a relational commitment. It is a commitment based on a personal relationship developed with Jesus, with the leader and with others in the small group. The "safe" atmosphere of the small group (mentioned in 11a) comes from the trust relationships built between the disciple and the leader and to a lesser extent between the disciple and other group members. The leader needs to create an atmosphere of grace—an environment in which there is an assurance of receiving love and where confidentiality is maintained so that there can be honesty about struggles and problems. As the leader gets to know the disciple, she will begin to see emotional and relational problems (if any). As trust develops, the leader can begin to gently expose them. If they are severe, she can help the disciple find help.

Foundational Truths (C) Disciple Builder:

12a   Teaches about the person and work of Christ: deity, authority, power, sovereignty, Lordship.

12b   Shares how to walk daily with Christ: importance of obedience, daily acceptance by grace, role and work of the Holy Spirit, spiritual disciplines, basic principles of divine guidance.

12c   Shows in Scripture that Christ is the intercessor and helper for all needs.

12d   Shares how to deal with emotions (past and present).

12e   Helps disciple develop a better understanding that God created people with needs and emotions.

Disciple Builder: The foundation of the rest of the disciple's Christian life is her personal relationship with Jesus. Therefore, it is important to go through content slowly enough for her to apply the truths she is learning. It is tempting to study material (information) and then go on to the next topic without waiting for God the Holy Spirit to use time and circumstances to make the truths real in daily life.

Regarding teaching on the Holy Spirit, the emphasis here should be on the role of the Spirit (as the source of power, the fruit of the Spirit, etc.) in the Christian's growth process, not on the spiritual gifts.

Cultivates Relationships with God and Christians (A) Disciple:

13a   Is regularly involved with Christian activities: accepts small tasks within the body, seeks fellowship with Christians.

13b   Is committed to a small group Bible study, open to correction.

Exhibit 3

13c Is developing a growing relationship with Jesus: is cultivating a daily quiet time (prayer, Bible study, Scripture memory, etc.), is seeking to walk obediently with Christ daily, is talking with others about Jesus and is growing in sensitivity to sin.

13d Is developing an awareness of own emotional issues and is willing to work on them.

Disciple Builder: The definition of "committed" here means to attend faithfully, complete brief homework assignments and meet occasionally with the leader. Commitment at the beginning of the small group may be less than this; however, the disciple should be growing toward this commitment. At this point in the disciple's growth, the leader should be available to answer questions and help with faith steps, but not crowd the disciple or try to force growth. Be careful not to require (expect) too much commitment too soon. Your level of commitment to the disciple needs to reflect the disciple's level of commitment.

As a disciple builder, realize that disciples do not all grow at the same rate. Based on emotional maturity, personality and personal circumstances, growth rates will vary. Learn to be comfortable with (and sensitive to) the fact that growth in an individual, and therefore in a group, will not be orderly nor perfectly predictable. Guidelines presented here are just that—guidelines, not rigid standards.

You know that a disciple is becoming a "Ministry Trainee" (Phase III: Equipping For Ministry) when she exhibits the traits and habits listed in "A" (Accountability) consistently. These are evidence of a strong personal relationship with Christ, which is the critical foundational need at this point. To hurry the development of this relationship is a mistake. Remember that Christlike character as well as conduct is the goal—not just doing the right things, but being a "virtuous" person and turning away from sin as a lifestyle.

Understanding and Growth (P) Disciple Builder prays:

14a For disciple to understand who Jesus is, what He has done and how to walk with Him, and to begin to meet with Christ in a daily quiet time (John 6:44; Ephesians 1:18-22).

14b   For personal needs in disciple's life, for disciple's growth in dependence on Jesus to meet personal needs, to see Jesus work in day-to-day life.

14c   For disciple to continue to turn from old lifestyle, establish new habits, experience Christian fellowship, develop a seriousness about God's will and Word.

14d   For disciple to develop healthy ways of dealing with emotions and getting needs met.

Involvement in Body of Christ (S) Disciple:

15a   Is allowed to observe leader in relationship with God and in ministry situations; disciple meets with leader periodically.

15b   Is asked to help with tasks (especially physical tasks, not tasks that require spiritual experience and maturity). Is asked to get involved in the body of Christ.

15c   Attends small group Bible study and/or a Restoring Your Heart group (if applicable).

Exhibit 3

Phase III: Equipping For Ministry

Mentoring (R) Disciple Builder:

16a   Chooses a select, open group of disciples. New people may be added, but group membership is by invitation only. Group is used as a filtering process to determine who should be appointed leaders later.

16b   Meets regularly with the disciple to apply basic ministry skill material (especially "P"—Participation of OPSI), to develop a good personal relationship and to hold each other accountable for personal and spiritual goals.

16c   Encourages disciple to establish casual friendships with non-Christians and to grow in commitment to other Christians (in social situations, service activities, projects, etc.).

16d   Encourages disciple to learn relational principles and skills.

Law and Grace (C) Disciple Builder:

17a   Trains disciple in basic ministry skills: evangelism, testimony preparation, inductive Bible study, time management and healthy relationships.

17b   Teaches disciple about nature of God's Kingdom: benefits of Christ's redemptive work (deliverance from disease, demons and death, forgiveness of sin, justification by faith and freedom from the law), the power and leadership of Holy Spirit, spiritual warfare and walking by grace (not under law).

17c   Teaches disciple the vision of discipleship. Emphasizes balance between evangelism and service, adapting the gospel, and the priority of ministry (balance).

17d   Teaches disciple how to develop healthy relationships.

Disciple Builder: Remember that the truth Christ taught His disciples often unfolded in stages throughout the growth process. This is true in the area of spiritual warfare. At the Ministry Trainee level (Phase III: Equipping For Ministry), you need to focus on the fact that there are opposing forces in our world, the sources of those forces, the supremacy of Christ in the warfare and the weapons of warfare Christians have.

Becomes Ministry-Minded (A) Disciple:

18a   Begins to minister to those around him: takes responsibility for tasks within the ministry ("P"—Participation—part of OPSI) and shares Christ with others (including testimony and follow-up).

18b   Actively takes a stand for the gospel by sharing his faith and by being identified with Christians.

18c   Makes ministry a priority: develops Christian friends to minister with, is accountable to leader (ministry trainer), is a faithful member of group designed to teach ministry skills and develops a vision for discipleship.

18d   Develops healthy relationships and proper boundaries in ministry endeavors.

Disciple Builder: Part of the purpose of taking responsibility for tasks within the ministry is to give the disciple an opportunity to try different areas of ministry to discover his spiritual gifts. The phrase "being identified with Christians" in 18b does not refer to the fact that a disciple needs to be publicly identified with Christ through baptism. (Ideally, this faith step already was taken when the disciple became a Christian.) It does refer to the disciple actively taking a stand for the gospel by sharing his faith, giving a personal testimony, being identified with a Christian ministry, etc.

When a disciple understands how to develop healthy relationships, he does not force the gospel on others and does not try to manipulate a response to the gospel. He also knows how to maintain healthy

Exhibit 3

boundaries in ministry so he doesn't allow others to take advantage of his time and resources.

When a disciple exhibits the elements listed above in "A" (Accountability), he is showing evidence of being ready to be appointed as a "New Leader" (Phase IV: Developing New Leaders). As before, remember that growth is more than just doing activities. In addition to doing the right activities, there needs to be growth in godly character. In this Phase, there is an emphasis on having a correct assessment of and perspective on the spiritual world.

Courage and Provision (P) Disciple Builder prays:

19a   That disciple sees the priority of ministry, grows in desire for ministry, and has opportunities to minister and grow in commitment to the body (Luke 5:8-10).

19b   That disciple understands Jesus' power to forgive (Luke 5:16-26).

19c   That there will be an open door for gospel, that disciple will develop a burden for the lost and become bold in his witness.

19d   That disciple understands that having healthy relationships is a priority if he is to be effective in ministry.

Opportunity to Serve and Witness (S) Disciple:

20a   Accepts small challenges in ministry (Does "P"—Participation—part of OPSI).

20b   Is in a Ministry Training group.

20c   Attends a short-term mission project.

20d   Learns about ministry relationships from a variety of ministry opportunities.

Phase IV: Developing New Leaders

PART A—APPOINTING NEW LEADERS

Training (R) Disciple Builder:

21a   Chooses select, closed group of disciples (for leadership group).

21b   Encourages strong commitments among this group of disciples.

21c   Meets regularly with disciple and continues to be a model for her.

Disciple Builder: Choosing leaders is a critical event in the life of a group as well as in the lives of disciples. Be sure to apply biblical qualifications—especially godly character—as you evaluate (qualities in the Sermon on the Mount). Jesus spent all night in prayer before choosing The Twelve. Thus, we need to follow His example and seek God diligently and humbly when choosing leaders.

There are some common mistakes to avoid when appointing leaders. First, do not appoint people as leaders before they have had enough time and opportunity to demonstrate faithfulness. The leader needs to observe and interact with the disciple over time. On the other hand, do not wait too long to give developing leaders responsibilities. We all grow by being challenged! Obviously, a balance is needed: prayer and careful discernment are necessary. Also, if there are no people to lead, do not appoint leaders.

Leadership Principles: Character, Authority (C) Disciple Builder:

22a   Teaches Sermon on the Mount. Includes topics such as Christian character, ethical conduct, meaning of heart obedience, true worship, eternal perspective on issues in culture, and parables of the Kingdom (Matthew 13).

Exhibit 3

22b   Teaches Parables of the Kingdom including extending the kingdom to others, conflict with Satan's kingdom (spiritual warfare), and growth of the Kingdom.

22c   Teaches about discipleship in the family, spiritual gifts, discipleship philosophy (an overview), and ministry to the hurting (healing).

Disciple Builder: The concept of the "Kingdom" and Christians as "Kingdom people" is a theme at this point and should be emphasized. Disciples should be encouraged to try different ministry situations with the goal of discovering their spiritual gifts. New leaders should be learning to identify emotional problems and how to help others begin to heal.

Assumes Leadership Responsibilities (A) Disciple:

23a   Has a personal ministry ("S"—Supervision—of OPSI): assumes responsibility and leadership in ministry, grows in her ability to study the Bible (inductive Bible study and special literature like Parables), and faithfully shares the gospel.

23b   Has a consistent walk with God, exhibits godly character (Sermon on the Mount) and grows in dependence on God.

23c   Takes bold stands on spiritual and moral issues.

Disciple Builder: Realize that your disciple, a new leader, has needs and areas to continue to grow in and does not have experience to draw from. Therefore you may need to drop back to the "P" phase of OPSI in an area to meet a need she has. When a disciple exhibits the elements listed above in "A" (Accountability), she is showing evidence of being ready to move on to the stage of Phase IV: Developing New Leaders—Part B. Again, the emphasis is not on living the Christian life perfectly, but on general growth progressing toward Christlike maturity.

Perspective and Wisdom (P) Disciple Builder prays:

24a   For discernment in selection of new leaders.

24b   For disciples (new leaders) to have an effective ministry to others. Prays that there are new disciples for new leaders to lead, that disciples are able to see potential in younger Christians, and that disciples are strengthened by the Holy Spirit.

24c   For disciples to continue to grow in godly character, to be obedient to the principles in Sermon on Mount, and to be protected from the evil one (especially from spiritual pride).

Appointment to Leadership Roles (S) Disciple:

25a   Participates in leadership group (retreats, meetings, etc.) and in mission projects (short-term, domestic and overseas).

25b   Meets regularly with leader for accountability, encouragement and instruction.

25c   Has a personal ministry ("S"—Supervision—of OPSI) and provides leadership in the movement.

PART B—FOCUSING ON ETERNAL THINGS

Encouraging (R) Disciple Builder:

26a   Continues with select, closed group chosen in Phase IV-A, and builds intimate relationships.

26b   Models transparency.

26c   Makes sure that disciple has a personal ministry with Christians being equipped for ministry ("S"—Supervision—of OPSI).

Exhibit 3

Eternal Perspective (C) Disciple Builder:

27a   Teaches disciples to reevaluate their world view: eternal values
      are superior to temporal ones (Philippians 1:12-14,18). This
      includes racial and cross-cultural issues, materialism, legalism,
      etc.

27b   Teaches about Christ's sufficiency: His provision enables us
      to do whatever He demands. Victory in spiritual battle comes
      only by the Holy Spirit.

27c   Teaches about sovereignty of God: how to follow divine
      authority over human tradition, about biblical authority and
      how it should be administered, and about the openness of the
      kingdom to all (universal nature of the church).

27d   Teaches about having realistic biblical expectations for
      Christian growth and development. Teaches about how to
      "sort out good and bad." (That is, teaches disciple how to
      emotionally live with the simultaneous existence of good and
      bad in herself, in others and in our world.)

Disciple Builder: The theme of "eternal vs. temporal" values affects
many areas of a disciple's life in addition to the ones listed in 27a. The
general principle is that daily life is filled with choices—how to spend
money, where to live, where to work, etc.—and eternal values need to
be the guide for decision-making rather that temporal ones.

Regarding 27d: included here is a theology of suffering. How does
a Christian deal with hard times, illnesses, disappointments, failure,
etc.? Too often, Christian culture does not address these issues, and
thus seems to imply that they do not exist for the Christian. A related
issue is the fact that as Christians we live in a state of "now but not
yet"—the kingdom has come on earth through and in us, and yet, at
the same time, the kingdom is still in the future.

Adjusts Expectations (A) Disciple:

28a   Rejects worldly values and embraces eternal values.

28b   Submits to biblical authorities and to Word of God (over the word of men).

28c   Lives in a way that reflects God's grace and obedience rather than a rewards/punishment mind-set.

28d   Has realistic view of the world and herself as being both good and bad. Is able to give herself and others grace.

Disciple Builder: When a disciple exhibits the elements listed above in "A" (Accountability), she is showing evidence of being ready to move on to the stage of Phase V: Developing Mature Leaders—Part A. The disciple continues to have a ministry.

Endurance (P) Disciple Builder prays:

29a   That disciple will be discerning and live for eternal values.

29b   That disciple will see the glorified Christ—His authority on earth and in heaven.

29c   That disciple will have understanding in spiritual battles.

29d   That disciple has an accurate view of God, self and others.

Acceptance of Difficult Assignments (S) Disciple:

30a   Participates in leadership group (retreats, meetings, etc.) and in mission projects (short-term, domestic and overseas).

30b   Meets regularly with the leader for accountability, encouragement and instruction.

30c   Participates in evangelistic outreaches to new classes of people.

Exhibit 3

Disciple Builder: It is important that content in this section be taught in an atmosphere of grace and encouragement. Many of the topics deal with principles of lifestyle (how much is enough, living a simple life, etc.), and an improper emphasis on these topics can develop. Some people tend to drift toward the extreme of asceticism in which there is a belief that it is "more spiritual" to do without and to judge people who don't agree. Be sensitive to this danger.

Phase V: Developing Mature Leaders

PART A—DELEGATING NEW RESPONSIBILITIES

Delegating (R) Disciple Builder:

31a Continues with select, closed group chosen in Phase IV-A, and continues to build intimate relationships.

31b Models suffering love to disciples (leadership team).

31c Also, models loyalty and faithfulness to disciples (leadership team).

Team Ministry (C) Disciple Builder:

32a Models and teaches: unity and harmony in the body of Christ; discipline in the body of Christ; reconciliation of brother in sin; and trust in Christ to work in other members of the body (Romans 14).

32b Models and teaches how to deal with conflicts outside the body regarding false religions and opposition from Christians outside the group.

32c Teaches team leadership and delegation of responsibility, and develops ministries related to spiritual gifts and calling.

Fosters Unity (A) Disciple:

33a Willingly forgives an offending brother.

33b Trusts God to work through others in the midst of disagreements.

33c Submits to difficult authorities without compromising truth.

33d Helps give leadership to the overall ministry and to a specialized ministry related to gifting.

Exhibit 3

Disciple Builder: When disciples exhibit the elements listed above in "A" (Accountability), they are showing evidence of being ready to move on to the stage of Phase V: Developing Mature Leaders–Part B. Other qualities that will be evident are an ability to delegate (trust God to work in and through others), to confront sin and to grow in unselfishness.

Unity in Diversity (P) Disciple Builder prays:

34a That disciple will have a burden for intercessory prayer.

34b That disciple will deal with confrontation in the body in a biblical way (Matthew 18:15-21).

34c That disciple will be bold and be protected from Satan's attacks and criticism.

34d That disciple will remain humble and learn to serve those he is leading

Ability to Work with Other Leaders (S) Disciple:

35a Participates in the leadership group (retreats, meetings, etc.).

35b Meets regularly with the leader for accountability, encouragement and instruction.

35c Provides leadership in the overall movement.

Disciple Builder: A pitfall at this point is to fail to give the mature leader increasing responsibility and decision-making authority. A disciple needs to be operating relatively independently in his ministry with occasional check-in points for accountability and advice. In contrast, the personal relationship with the disciple deepens and grows in commitment.

PART B—CASTING A WORLD VISION

Commissioning (R) Disciple Builder:

36a Continues with select, closed group. Helps them build intimate relationships. Has disciples participate on a leadership team.

36b Is sure that disciple's relationship with him is primarily a peer relationship.

36c Perseveres in difficult relationships.

Resurrection Power in Daily Life (C) Disciple Builder:

37a Teaches all-sufficiency of Christ as He ministered and rested in the power of the Spirit rather than in the flesh. Also teaches about spiritual warfare and dependent prayer.

37b Teaches and models sacrificial nature of leadership: throne perspective (i.e., all things are ours, so give up the world) and love, as the mark of the Christian.

37c Teaches about developing a world vision and about personal responsibility to spread the gospel.

Disciple Builder: You as the leader may need to help the disciple articulate specific goals for ministry.

Show Sacrificial Love to Reach the World (A) Disciple:

38a Trusts and rests in the Spirit alone in spite of circumstances. Consistently desires to show suffering love.

38b Lives life characterized by dependent prayer.

38c Has a ministry vision and a world vision.

Exhibit 3

Disciple Builder: It is important to help the disciple avoid the danger of self-confident professionalism, i.e., trusting abilities, especially ministry abilities, instead of God.

Sacrificial Love (P) Disciple Builder prays:

39a   That disciple understands that ministry can be carried out only in the power of the Holy Spirit.

39b   That Holy Spirit works in lives as gospel is proclaimed.

39c   That disciple and his ministry are protected from power of Satan.

Acceptance of Worldwide Challenge (S) Disciple:

40a   Takes leadership in the movement.

40b   Functions independently from leader.

40c   Attends and/or organizes prayer meetings for empowering disciples to be Christ's witnesses.

Disciple Building: A Biblical Framework
Guided Discussions

Table Of Contents

Chapter 1	The Priority Of Christlike Maturity	135
Chapter 2	Phases Of Growth	139
Chapter 3	The Five Initiatives	143
Chapter 4	What Jesus Did, What We Can Do	147
Chapter 5	Emotional Healing	151
Chapter 6	Balance Is Required	155
Answers To The Guided Discussions		159

Guided Discussion
The Priority Of Christlike Maturity—#1

Before attending this session, read Chapters 1-5 in *Disciple Building: A Biblical Framework*

GOAL:

To help the disciple understand the biblical basis for Biblical Truth #1 and #2 of *A Biblical Framework*.

GETTING STARTED:

What happens in a business if the leadership is not mature?

Transition: In the same way, spiritual immaturity in church leaders has a negative effect on the functioning of the church.

STUDYING TOGETHER:

1. According to the *Framework* what is a major problem facing the church today?

    Share an example.

Read Matthew 28:18-20.

2. What mandate did Jesus give to His leaders (the disciples)?

3. How could this mandate impact this character crisis?

4. How can a leader teach in such a way that the hearers actually apply the truth?

Read Ezra 7:6,10-11, 9:1-15, 10:1-6.

5. What do we know about Ezra from these passages?

6. How was Ezra able to impact all the Israelites?

7. According to the *Framework*, why has the church been weak on sanctification?

LOOKING AT REAL LIFE:

8. Have you seen spiritual immaturity in church leaders lead to problems in the church, both the church worldwide and the local church? Explain.

9. Have you seen people of godly character impact the church for good? Explain.

LOOKING AT MY LIFE:

Have leaders of the church influenced you? Explain.

Guided Discussion
Phases Of Growth—#2

Before attending this session, read Chapters 6-7 and the first two sections of Addendum A in *Disciple Building: A Biblical Framework*.

GOAL:

To help the disciple gain an overview of the Five Phases of Christ's ministry and develop a more complete understanding of Phase II.

GETTING STARTED:

What are some of the characteristics of a successful franchise?

Transition: In the same way, Jesus gave His church a pattern/model for discipleship to help Christians become more Christlike.

STUDYING TOGETHER:

Read Matthew 28:20.

1. In this verse, what are the indicators that we should follow His pattern?

2. Referring to "The Five Phases Of Disciple Building" in Chapter 7, in groups of two or three, briefly summarize what Christ did and taught at each Phase.

   Phase I:

   Phase II:

   Phase III:

   Phase IV:

   Phase V:

3. From Addendum A, what are the key emphases in Phase II?

LOOKING AT REAL LIFE:

4. Based on your answer to question #3 what could you do to help a person grow as a young disciple?

5. Who do you know that could benefit from receiving help going through Phase II? Explain.

6. What do you think the impact would be on the church if Christians really had a good understanding of God's character and how to grow spiritually?

LOOKING AT MY LIFE:

What was your experience as a young believer? Was there a specific person who helped you begin to grow? Were you in a small group for young believers?

OR

If you weren't in a small group or didn't have a specific person helping you grow, what contributed most to your growth?

The Five Initiatives—#3

Before attending this session, read Chapter 8, Addendum B, Exhibit 2, and the pages for Phase II of Exhibit 3 in *Disciple Building: A Biblical Framework.*

GOAL:

To help the disciple understand the five initiatives of a disciple builder and how to apply them to a Phase II believer.

GETTING STARTED:

What are the essential parts of a mouse trap that enable it to work?

What would happen if there were no "hammer" on the mouse trap?

What if there was no hold-down bar?

Transition: In discipleship there are several essential elements that must be present for it (the discipleship) to be effective.

STUDYING TOGETHER:

1. Briefly describe the five major elements or initiatives that must be present for discipleship to be successful.

    Five Initiatives:

    Relationship:

Content:

Accountability:

Prayer:

Situations (Structures):

2. Explain what the result would be if an initiative were missing.

Relationship:

Content:

Accountability:

Prayer:

Situations:

3. List and describe each of the steps of transfer, OPSI (beginning of Addendum B). Give an example of how the steps of transfer have worked in your experience or in that of someone you know.

O:

P:

S:

I:

It's important for you to understand the relationship between the Grid (Exhibit 2) and the Legend (Exhibit 3). The numbers in the middle of each square of the Grid correspond to the relevant information in the Legend. (The Legend is meant to show many of the disciple building activities, but not all of them.)

4. Using the R-CAPS Grid and Legend...

...if the disciple is in Phase II, what should be the Relationship emphasis?

...if the disciple is in Phase II, what should be the Content emphasis?

...if the disciple is in Phase II, what should be the Accountability emphasis?

...if the disciple is in Phase II, what should be the Prayer emphasis?

...if the disciple is in Phase II, what should be the Situations (structures) emphasis?

LOOKING AT REAL LIFE:

5. Imagine that you are discipling "Jim" or "Suzy." This person needs to grow in his/her personal relationship with God. To meet this need, you want to teach the person how to have a quiet time. Write a plan about how you will help the disciple accomplish this goal using each of the initiatives.

R:

C:

A:

P:

S:

LOOKING AT MY LIFE:

How do you think understanding the Phases and Initiatives will help you as you disciple others?

What Jesus Did, What We Can Do—#4

Before attending this session, read Exhibit 1 of *Disciple Building: A Biblical Framework*.

GOAL:

To help the disciple understand more about the Five Phases of growth, the Five Initiatives and how these can be reproduced in our ministries.

GETTING STARTED:

Why is it important that we study history?

Transition: We have the amazing opportunity to look at the ministry of Jesus Christ Himself, and we need to carefully observe how He discipled The Twelve.

STUDYING TOGETHER:

1. What are some of the things that stand out to you about what Jesus did in His ministry? Explain.

2. What are some of the things that stand out to you as you read the *What We Can Do* column? Explain.

147

The following passages describe things Jesus did in Phase II.

Read John 1:29-51.

3. What did Jesus accomplish while gathering His disciples in this passage?

4. What did He model in this passage?

Read John 2:1-11.

5. How did this experience with Jesus affect His disciples?

6. What did He model in this passage?

Read John 4:1-26.

7. What did Jesus' disciples learn about evangelism from His experience with the woman at the well?

8. What did He model in this passage?

LOOKING AT REAL LIFE:

9. What are some things we can do in ministry that will help younger Christians understand the principles Jesus demonstrated in these verses?

LOOKING AT MY LIFE:

Write down one thing you can do this week to encourage a young believer.

Emotional Healing—#5

Before attending this session, read Addendum C in *Disciple Building: A Biblical Framework*.

GOAL:

To help the disciple understand the role of emotional healing in discipleship.

GETTING STARTED:

Imagine that you are putting together a 500-piece jigsaw puzzle. There is no picture on the box to refer to, and several key pieces are missing. In fact, some of the missing pieces belong to a person's face, obscuring their identity. Having these pieces missing prevents you from visualizing the whole picture that the artist had in mind.

Have you been in a situation in which you couldn't solve a problem or a dilemma because you were "missing" puzzle pieces—that is, all the information you needed? Explain; give examples.

Transition: Often there are "missing pieces" in a Christian's spiritual life that hinder spiritual growth. One of these "missing pieces" in discipleship can be emotional healing.

STUDYING TOGETHER:

1. If a person failed to complete one of the developmental tasks, there can be problems in adulthood. Consider each task: Bonding, Separating, Sorting Out Good and Bad and Gaining Independence, and explain the problems that might be faced in adulthood if a task is incomplete.

151

Bonding:

Separation:

Sorting Out Good And Bad:

Gaining Independence:

2. Read the list of goals in Addendum C for Phase II (Laying Foundations).

What do you think the personal consequences might be if someone does NOT complete goal #2, i.e. doesn't develop self awareness?

What do you think the personal consequences would be if someone does NOT complete goal #7, identify and learn to deal with emotions appropriately?

What do you think the personal consequences might be if a person does NOT complete goal #8, understand grieving and forgiveness?

LOOKING AT REAL LIFE:

3. What may be some of the advantages of a church that stresses emotional healing over a church that doesn't?

LOOKING AT MY LIFE:

As you read the information about developmental tasks, what statement caught your attention and made you think, "Wow, that's me!"? Explain.

Is there anyone in your past that hurt you that you have not forgiven? Explain without using the person's name.

Balance Is Required—#6

Before attending this session, read Chapter 9 in *Disciple Building: A Biblical Framework*.

GOAL:

To help the disciple understand the importance of maintaining balance in both theology and in practice in disciple building.

GETTING STARTED:

A person can get off-balance in some area of her life. What are some of the results in the lives of people who have gotten out of balance by focusing on an extreme idea? (E.g. extreme: in health, diet, politics, religion, education)

Transition: In discipleship, it is essential to stay in balance and avoid extremes. In this lesson we will look at several discipleship ideas that need to be kept in balance.

STUDYING TOGETHER:

1. Briefly summarize each of the 6 areas the *Framework* addresses in this chapter that require balance:

   Divine Initiative And Human Responsibility:

   Positional And Experiential Truth:

World Evangelization And Disciple Building:

Different Settings And Structures For Growth:

Disciple Building And Leadership:

Leader Development And Emotional Healing:

2. Think of an example in each of the six areas of how balance was not kept.

    Divine Initiative And Human Responsibility:

    Positional And Experiential Truth:

    World Evangelization And Disciple Building:

    Different Settings And Structures For Growth:

    Disciple Building And Leadership:

Leader Development And Emotional Healing:

LOOKING AT REAL LIFE:

3. From your perspective evaluate your own church and assess how it is doing with respect to these 6 areas. (The purpose of this question is not to gossip about or slander your church. The purpose is for you to evaluate and consider helpful remedies.)

4. What could your church do to improve in one or more of these areas?

LOOKING AT MY LIFE:

In your personal ministry, in regard to these areas of balance, what do you think are your strengths? Your weaknesses?

What can you do to shore up your weaknesses?

Answers To The Guided Discussions

Leaders should read the Leader's Instructions For Using Guided Discussions, located at the beginning of the book, before facilitating a small group. Leaders also need to read the following notes and answers before the meeting where the specific lesson will be discussed. Here they will find suggestions, cautions and additional helpful information.

1 The Priority Of Christlike Maturity—#1

GETTING STARTED: *In general, a business would be run poorly and may not be successful. The leaders will tend to be selfish and not consider long-term effects of decisions on employees. Are more concerned about themselves than the good of the company and the good of the employees. Tend to emphasize bureaucracy rather than relationships. Leaders tend to have poor problem solving skills, might try to take short cuts. Leaders try to get around the law or take advantage of all loopholes. Take credit for what others do.*

1. *Crisis of character*

3. a) *People would become Christians, disciples of Christ, and be changed on the inside.*

   b) *People could become part of the church (fellowship of believers) so they can learn how to walk as a Christian, learn how to have a relationship with Christ.*

   c) *People could grow in Christlikeness as leaders taught and applied everything that Jesus taught.*

   d) *As people become mature Christians they have an impact on the world.*

4. *There should be prayer, healthy relationships where there is modeling of truth, accountability and encouragement. The leader can craft situations that will help the hearer apply truth. There must also be good biblical teaching.*

5. *He was a leader in Babylon among the Israelites and was schooled in the Law of Moses. He was a priest, taught the law, and his relationship with God was strong. He also got permission from the king to go to Jerusalem.*

6. *He impacted them through the expression of his character. When he was told about their sin, he didn't lecture them. Instead, he humbled himself before God and repented for the sins of the people. As a result, conviction fell on the people.*

7. *The Protestant Reformation primarily focused on justification by faith, not works. It did not focus as much on the development of Christian character (sanctification.) As a result, the evangelical church continues to be more concerned about salvation than about sanctification.*

2 Phases Of Growth

GETTING STARTED: *Franchises can be reproduced over and over again because the leaders of the corporation provide a pattern/model to be followed by the franchise operators. Therefore, franchises are very similar to each other. However, there is some flexibility in order to allow the franchise to meet specific needs. The franchise operators have the help of the leaders to reproduce the model.*

1. *He gave us the command to repeat what Christ has done. Also, He promises to be with us even to the end of the age which indicates His intention that we continue building until He returns.*

2. Phase I: *The emphasis is on our need for salvation and our call to repentance and faith. New believers need to be followed up by continuing to reinforce the truths surrounding salvation.*

   Phase II: *The disciples lived in community with Jesus and developed a close personal relationship with Him. He revealed who He was (Messiah and Son of God) and His power (through miracles). They learned to trust and follow Him obediently. Through modeling, He taught them how to relate to each other and how to begin to share their faith.*

Phase III: *Jesus called some of his disciples to be "fishers of men." He took them with him in his evangelistic campaigns, and taught them the principles of evangelism. He demonstrated His love for the sinner and His power to forgive sin, give new life. He began teaching them about the two spiritual kingdoms.*

Phase IV: *He appointed The Twelve disciples as leaders (apostles). He taught them kingdom principles (in the Sermon on the Mount), and how His Kingdom would grow (in the Parables). He taught them principles of spiritual warfare and showed them how to cast out demons. He also sent them out two-by-two. By doing this, Jesus precipitated a crisis forcing the disciples to reevaluate their expectations about the Christian life.*

Phase V: *As The Twelve assumed increased responsibility for the ministry, they became self-reliant. They began to trust their own efforts and had to learn (through the crucifixion and resurrection) that human efforts are not adequate to live the Christian life. They also learned that Jesus worked through all members of the body and that they needed to be able to deal with outside opposition. Other events helped the disciples learn about God's sovereignty and His all-sufficiency. Before He left, Jesus gave the disciples a worldwide vision and commissioned them to make disciples. He challenged them to repeat what He taught them, and in turn, told them to urge their disciples to do the same.*

3. *Gain a better understanding of who Jesus is.
    *Build a relationship with Christ.
    *Learn how to obey and follow Him.
    *Experience Jesus meeting their needs and answering their prayers.
    *Experience community in a small group.

4. *Have the young believer read a Gospel (especially John)*
   Teach a person to have a quiet time.
   Have a young believer identify personal needs and pray for specific needs.
   Join a small group that's focused on how to live the Christian life or that's focused on the character of God

3 The Five Initiatives

GETTING STARTED: *Platform, hold-down bar, the hammer, a spring and a trigger (catch). Mouse wouldn't be caught. The trap couldn't be set.*

1. Relationship: *Connect in such a way that a disciple knows that you love and care for him and trust is built*

   Content: *Appropriate content taught from the Word and applied (obeyed).*

   Accountability: *Builds from a relationship that is encouraging, helpful and focused on applying specific truths and skills. Appropriate pressure is loving and wise.*

   Prayer: *Pray for understanding and application of truth.*

   Situations (Structures): *Specific situations that facilitate spiritual growth*

2. Relationship: *Discipleship would be demotivating and lack the advantages of modeling.*

   Content: *Discipleship would not have biblical, solid truth to teach.*

   Accountability: *There would be a lack of progress in growth; lack of clarity; no encourager*

   Prayer: *Lack of prayer would create an atmosphere of pride and independence, and focus attention on man, not God.*

Situations: *Without appropriate teaching situations a disciple would not learn how to transfer to real life.*

3. O: *Observation: Disciple watches as another person performs an activity*

    P: *Participation: Disciple participates with another in the activity*

    S: *Supervision: Disciple builder supervises the disciple doing the activity*

    I: *Independence: Disciple does activity on his own*

4. *A nurturing, caring relationship with a disciple builder and other Christians in a safe small group*

    Disciple learns foundational principles about the Christian life: who Christ is; how to have a relationship with Him and how to follow Him

    Helping a disciple to apply the truths of Phase II

    Pray that the disciple understands truth and learns how to apply it, and gets excited about his growth in Christ

    Become involved in activities in the body of Christ

4 What Jesus Did, What We Can Do

GETTING STARTED: *So we won't repeat the errors of the past, to discover what works and what doesn't work, to learn from great minds of the past, to gain perspective, etc.*

3. *He invited them to be with Him. ("Come and see.") He convinced them that He is Messiah. He welcomed other men who were interested in the Messiah into His group. He formed a small group of followers. He spoke prophetic words to Nathaniel, therefore showing that He had prophetic abilities. He spoke positive and encouraging words to His group of followers about who they were and who*

they were to become. He changed Peter's name according to the potential He saw in Peter.

4. *He did the following things with the goal of showing His followers how they should live and minister. He exhibited a positive attitude toward those who were His followers and He wanted them to do the same with their followers. He was warm and welcoming to His followers as a model for them to their followers. He indicated that His followers had the potential for playing a significant role in His Kingdom. He formed personal relationships with His followers and provided the opportunity for them to form relationships with each other.*

5. *They became closer to Him as they spent time with Him. Because of this miracle the disciples' faith in Him increased. When He turned water into wine (which was the first sign through which He revealed His glory) they became more convinced that He was the Messiah. They observed that everywhere He went He made a positive difference.*

6. *He modeled humility and compassion. He rescued the hosts from embarrassment by providing the wine they needed. Spoke honestly to His mother.*

7. *They learned that Jesus was concerned about the salvation of everyone. They learned that He was willing to break cultural norms in order to reach people.*

8. *He gained the Samaritan woman's attention in a creative way. He answered her questions, exposed her sin, gave her hope. He made it clear that He was the Messiah. He understood where she was spiritually and helped her gain a clear understanding of salvation.*

5 Emotional Healing

1. Bonding: *If bonding doesn't occur the following messages are not internalized: I am loved; My feelings and needs are OK; I can trust others to meet my needs. When he becomes an adult the person*

will have problems connecting with other people because he cannot accept love, does not trust others and/or is out of touch with his own feelings and needs.

Separating: *If Separating doesn't occur in a child's life, as an adult he may face a general lack of self-understanding and direction, relational problems such as being too dependent on others, being too isolated from others, feeling too responsible for others, or becoming a caretaker. The person may develop significant boundary problems: allow others to take advantage of him, or he may take advantage of others.*

Sorting Out Good And Bad: *If a person doesn't complete this task, he tends to see things as all good or all bad. He cannot tolerate bad in himself or in others. He denies good, denies the bad or sees things as all good at first, and then all bad.*

Gaining Independence: *If a person doesn't complete this task he continues to depend on his parents, feels less mature than other adults, has inordinate need for approval, feels the need for permission to be granted before initiating action, feels inferior.*

2. *It might make it difficult to grow spiritually (it is hard to grow spiritually if you don't understand yourself); it might make it difficult to have purpose or direction in life if you don't understand your strengths, weaknesses, etc. It might be difficult to have healthy relationships (hard to get close to someone if you don't understand yourself so you can reveal who you are).*

    They may deny their emotions and let them build up inside until they explode. They might be controlled by their emotions and not express emotions in a healthy way. For example, they may make decisions based on their emotions that may lead to irrational emotions.

    If the person fails to grieve or is stuck in their grief, it inhibits their emotional growth and they can become bitter. The failure to forgive people gives them inappropriate control over the unforgiving person.

3. *A church that stresses emotional healing often has people who are able to have healthier relationships and healthier families. These people are able to express more understanding and grace to hurting people and help them heal. They are generally more honest with themselves and others. The church atmosphere is safe.*

   A church that doesn't stress emotional healing may have a tendency to ignore hurting people, may be legalistic (performance-oriented). May be more difficult to get to know people in the church. It may not be a safe environment to be honest about problems.

6 Balance Is Required

GETTING STARTED: *Person may experience isolation, see dissenters as the "enemy," be harsh and judgmental in attitude, have difficulty relating to people who don't agree, may be obnoxious and pushy, may develop "tunnel vision."*

1. Divine Initiative And Human Responsibility: *The role of man (human responsibility) and the role of God (divine initiative) in a person's life must both be a part of the growth process and be kept in balance.*

   Positional And Experiential Truth: *The believer's standing before God (positional truth) must be in balance with putting truth into action (experiential truth). If only one is emphasized it may lead to legalism or license.*

   World Evangelization And Disciple Building: *In history, at times, the church seems to focus mainly on evangelism, and at other times, seems to focus mainly on disciple building. There needs to be a balance between these two in order to produce healthy disciples and a healthy church.*

   Different Settings And Structures for Growth: *Jesus used different settings and different structures as He trained His disciples. We should follow His example. Different truths are best taught in different situations: small group, one-to-one, large group, etc.*

Disciple Building And Leadership: *In order to have healthy growth in a church there needs to be a focus on both building disciples and developing leaders. There needs to be a balance between these two elements.*

Leader Development And Emotional Healing: *Disciples need more than good teaching from the Bible in order to continue to grow. Good teaching is important, but many people come to Christ with "baggage" from the past: emotional and relational wounds. These wounds need to be healed or a disciple's spiritual development will slow or stop completely. The church must do both: leader development and emotional healing.*

About WDA

WDA's mission is to serve the church worldwide by developing Christlike character in people and equipping them to disciple others according to the pattern Jesus used to train His disciples.

Organized as Worldwide Discipleship Association (WDA) in 1974, we are based in the United States and have ministries and partners throughout the world. WDA is a 501c(3) non-profit organization funded primarily by the tax-deductible gifts of those who share our commitment to biblical disciple building.

WDA is committed to intentional, progressive discipleship. We offer a flexible, transferable approach that is based on the ministry and methods of Jesus, the Master Disciple Builder. By studying Jesus' ministry, WDA discovered five phases of Christian growth. The Cornerstone series focuses on the first and second phases, Phase I: Establishing Faith and Phase II: Laying Foundations. Cornerstone addresses the needs of a young Christian or a more mature Christian who wants a review of foundational Christian truths. The Equipping For Ministry phase (Phase III) is geared toward disciples who are ready to learn how to minister to others. Phase IV: Developing New Leaders equips a person to take responsibility for the spiritual development and well-being of others while Phase V: Developing Mature Leaders expands the training of mature leaders.

For more information about WDA and disciple building, please visit our website: www.disciplebuilding.org.

The following materials are available at the WDA store.
www.disciplebuilding.org/store

Maturity Matters®

Read *Maturity Matters®* by Bob Dukes.

Leaders must understand, balance, and apply the dynamics that contribute to progressive growth and sanctification. This requires both a strong faith and a new focus. As we fix our eyes on things unseen, the outcome will be a deeper faith, drawn in part from church leaders who consistently equip Christians. As we help them put truth into practice, faith grows. The rewards are both temporal and eternal.

Cornerstone

Begin to build disciples using Cornerstone.

WDA Cornerstone features 38 Bible lessons and essays that help new Christians grow to maturity. These lessons cover the first two phases of growth, Establishing Faith and Laying Foundations. The Cornerstone curriculum is designed to run for approximately one year. Once established, it runs continuously with various entry points. Ideally, it works in concert with Life Coaches, who meet with and help orient disciples to the Christian life and the church community, facilitating and supplementing their involvement in a Discipleship Community.

Life Coaching

Learn how to be a Life Coach.

Life Coaches are Christian leaders who are willing to invest their knowledge and experience and even their very lives so that others might learn to think, feel and act like Jesus. A spiritual Life Coach is a person who, in the midst of a caring relationship, imparts truth that changes the life (conduct/character) of another, gradually helping the disciple become more like Jesus Christ. At WDA, we often use the phrase, "meeting people where they are, helping them take the next step®" to describe the Life Coaching process. Life Coach training offers a philosophical and practical approach that is carried out through the design and implementation of growth projects tailored to individual needs and levels of maturity.

WDA is able to provide Life Coach training in three distinct ways: individual self-study using our *Disciple Building: Life Coaching* manual, group study and interaction at a Life Coaching Seminar or through a 28/20® church ministry consulting relationship. To learn more about Life Coaching go to www.disciplebuilding. org/ministries/church-ministry/life-coaching

Watch the Life Coaching Introductory Video: https:// vimeo.com/135056845

Phase III: Equipping For Ministry
Equip disciples to minister to others.

WDA's Equipping For Ministry consists of 7 workbooks and manuals that feature content focusing on character and skills. The topics in this phase can be approached individually or in sequence. Disciples will learn about healthy relationships, spiritual warfare, positional truth, ministry principles, evangelism and inductive Bible study.

At the Equipping For Ministry Phase (III) a disciple has a strong personal relationship with God and has matured to the point that he is ready to begin having a ministry in the life of another person. Training at this phase is best done in a team of disciples who learn and do ministry together with an experienced discipleship leader.

Restoring Your Heart

Read *How Emotional Problems Develop.*

Through our experiences discipling people over the years, we at WDA have discovered that unresolved relational and emotional issues from the past can be a stumbling block to spiritual growth.

Our Restorative Ministry trains people in churches and in other ministries to help people through a healing process that will enable them to become healthier in all their relationships, including their relationship with God.

Check out **Restoring Your Heart** at www.disciplebuilding.org/ministries/restorative-ministry.

WDA Partnerships

Help us build disciples worldwide.

You can help us fulfill the great commission by becoming a Worldwide Discipleship Association (WDA) partner. WDA's mission is to serve the church worldwide by developing Christlike character in people and equipping them to disciple others according to the pattern Jesus used to train His disciples.

Since our inception in 1974 our materials and processes have been used in more than 90 U.S. cities and in over 55 countries. We have created over a million direct discipleship impacts and have conducted face-to-face training to over 17,000 pastors and leaders around the globe! **Your support of WDA is vital to the success of our mission.** We pledge to serve as faithful stewards of your generous gifts to the ministry.

www.disciplebuilding.org/give/wda-partnership

Become a Partner Today

WDA®
Disciple Building

Made in the USA
Lexington, KY
06 December 2019